Mary lecoure (owner----
London 1994

Colin Spencer. Nov. 59.

Tom Burns

The Use
of Memory

Publishing and Further Pursuits

This is the use of memory:
For liberation – not less of love but expanding
Of love beyond desire, and so liberation
From the future as well as the past.

T. S. Eliot: *Little Gidding*

Sheed & Ward
London

ISBN 0–7220–9450–7

Published in Great Britain in 1993 by
Sheed & Ward Limited
14 Coopers Row
London EC3N 2BH

Production editor: Bill Ireson
Typeset: Waveney Typesetters, Norwich
Printed and bound in Great Britain by:
Biddles Limited, Guildford and King's Lynn

For Mabél Marañon, my wife,
for our children,
Maria-Belen, Tom, David and Jimmy,
and for our
eleven grandchildren

Acknowledgements

I would like to thank Mrs T. S. Eliot for permission to quote from *Little Gidding*. For deciphering my handwriting and providing me with an immaculate typescript I am indebted to Mrs Barbara (Lucas) Wall. My thanks, too, to Harman Grisewood for his invaluable comments whilst the work was in progress.

I am specially grateful to my publishers – where I learnt the gentle art some seventy years ago – for their care and interest.

Acknowledgement

Contents

List of Illustrations

Introduction

There is no excuse for an autobiography unless it contributes some mite of human experience to the whole, sheds a little light on an unfamiliar scene, shares something of value with its readers, or – at the very least – entertains them for a while. These are some uses of memory which, I hope, I have partially fulfilled.

An individual's life has only microscopic proportions, but it is precisely the microscope which has been the principal instrument of discovery in the natural world. By analogy, every human being reveals values in the world of spirit which escape measurement, being infinite. To realise this is the ultimate use of memory. So it has happened that, into a factual recall of events, which was my original intention in writing this book, there has intruded a certain current of thought without deliberation on my part.

It will become clear to readers that the Catholic faith which I received at baptism in my infancy has remained with me all the days of my life. I was undeniably polemical and a dogmatist in my youth, but to grow is to change, not to vacillate or attenuate but to develop conclusions from one's original premiss.

If, for instance, one's immature notion of conscience was simply of an occasional twinge of scrupulosity – which is an all-too common concept today – then one falls far short of a fundamental Christian concept. This is what Cardinal Newman expounded in his magisterial *Letter to the Duke of Norfolk* (first published in 1875) at a time when the authority of the Church and religion generally was being widely questioned. He was in no way belittling that authority but extolling conscience when he wrote:

> Certainly, if I am obliged to bring religion into after-dinner toasts (which indeed does not seem quite the thing) I shall drink to the Pope, if you please – still to conscience first and to the Pope afterwards.

I say Amen to that.

For Newman, and for the entire Christian tradition, conscience is virtually synonymous with consciousness of God's presence in the world and an understanding of what should flow from it in day-to-day living. Readers will be spared from having this view thrust upon them but it would be disingenuous if not dishonest on my part to cover it up.

They will also find no intimate revelations of men and women who have been specially close to me in one way or another. I once discussed this problem – inherent for any autobiographer – with Graham Greene. He summed up his view by saying, 'They have their own copyright.' I see what he meant. It is more than a technical or legal point. Any sort of relationship with another person is something shared so that to monopolise it is in effect to steal another's property.

I realise that what I have written touches no more than the tip of an iceberg. But I vouch for its being a fair sample of the whole. It is offered in thanksgiving for a lifetime of many surprises, of much work and much enjoyment and – above all – abundant friendship and love: *Ubi caritas et amor, ibi Deus est.*

T.F.B.
Mazagon, 1993

I

The Vanished World
of Wimbledon

I can't remember, can't remember, the house where I was born.
I am told that the year was 1906, and the place Viña del Mar in
Chile. I found my birthplace seventy years later when I went
back to Chile in search of my roots. Where the house and
garden had been stood a department store. Viña had been
shattered by the great earthquake of that year. But the parish
church had survived and there was my name in the register of
baptisms.

They tell me that in the first months of my existence I lived in
a tent made from a sheet of canvas draped over a pergola in the
rose garden. It was unsafe to go back to the house. When the
earthquake struck, it seems that I was in the drawing-room with
my *ama*. The plaster from the ceiling started to fall, so she got on
all fours and pushed me underneath her ample bosom. When
they found her and pulled her to her feet, her big flouncy skirt fell
away, weighed down with the plaster which would have buried
me. Beyond a bad bruising she was fine and nursed me for many
weeks in the pergola, our family camp.

Understandably I have no memory of that exciting time, but
memories of other people's memories have brought it all to life –
as well as myself to myself.

I was the seventh child of a man who had crossed the world
from his home in Brechin in the county of Angus in Scotland.
Like his four brothers, he had gone to the New World to seek a
livelihood. They all prospered in their various ways. The uncles,

like visiting planets, would recur in my boyhood – coming from the United States, Argentina and South Africa.

Uncle Walter was the eldest. He came from Portland, Oregon: a tall, slim, dignified figure, with his high cheek bones and sharp eyes. I took him to be a Red Indian. But now all that remains in my memory is his ponderous courtesy, staying on, when he disappeared, like the smile of the Cheshire Cat.

Uncle George had prospered on the Argentine pampas. He had a flamboyant moustache and the marks of smallpox on his sunburnt, ascetic face. When I was eight he called me his *secretario* and I learnt to buy his favourite brand of cigars at the local tobacconist in Wimbledon. He performed amazing feats with a lasso and was full of tales of *gaucho* life. I remember one in particular, when a drunken *gaucho* threatened his life. 'What did you do, *tio*?' I asked. 'I shot him like a dog.' Naturally *tio* went up in my estimation.

The third uncle was John who came from Boston. Plump and self-assured, he smoked endless cigars in an amber holder. I smoked one once in the lavatory and was very sick. I blamed myself for not having used an amber holder. He had a majestic open-topped Daimler with red leather seats and white-faced tyres. He was *en route* for retirement in Florence, like any other Bostonian, where he was converted to Dante and the Catholic Church.

Uncle Willie was the youngest, the poorest, and a poet. He was my mother's favourite and a constant irritant to my father. After a spell in India he had lived most of his life as a journalist in South Africa. At the outbreak of the Great War he enlisted in a Scottish regiment raised in Capetown. He entered my life at this point, in khaki and kilted, a big-boned lurching figure with faraway eyes, a quiet voice and a stammer which only left him when he recited poetry, his own or another's. He saw little, if any, active service and became one of the family through frequent visits, making poetic contributions to the family magazine, *The B-Hive*.

The avuncular planets heightened our existence in their

visiting but I think we were relieved when, one by one, they moved out of orbit. Uncle Willie retired to his birthplace in Brechin. He survived long enough to greet my wife, Mabél, and me by letter on our arrival from Spain in 1946. Typically he had dug out an old finely illustrated family history showing my forebears: a long line of bewigged divines, lawyers and soldiers. He inscribed it with a touching little poem to my wife, whom he never met. His two spinster sisters had long before declined to meet my mother, because she was a papist.

My father married Clara Swinburne in 1893. She was of English North Country stock but had been born and bred in Chile. I still have a faded photograph of her parents: he tall and straight with a grey top hat the height of a chimney and a grey frockcoat; she a little shrivelled woman in a shawl, with traces of her mother's strong Basque features – which persist in the family to this day. The British had a great presence in Chile at that time and now their blood has filtered down into countless families of Spanish origin. A spirit of moderation, a humane instinct and the work ethic of the British now mingles with the vitality and grace special to the Spaniards.

I see my destiny now in the predilections, tendencies, inclinations, habits and belief of this world of my childhood – and indeed in my children and grandchildren, reinforced in their case with a fresh influx of Spanish blood through my own marriage. Memory may fail us but we carry within us our past and every moment of it has been touched by all those of our blood who have gone before. None of us is an isolated individual. Even if one may never have known father or mother, or grandparents, they are all present in one's personality. And, of course, much more so when they actually inhabit and largely rule the world of one's childhood, as in my case.

The great Chilean earthquake of 1906 was the proximate cause of my parents' decision to pull out of the country and make for

London. The wrench must have been costing in many ways. My father was well established in banking; my mother, for all her north British forebears, was a passionate Chilean patriot. For many years, once in England, she would celebrate Chilean Independence day, 18 September, with her numerous Chilean friends in London. The President of Chile gave her the little table on which the actual Independence Treaty had been signed. She brought it to England and it is in my possession to this day. Her English was perfect although heavily accented and spiced with Spanish words. Her increasingly anglicised children would tease her about this. She had a Spaniard's indelible faith. She was devout without obtrusive piety. The Mass to her (as to all her children) was as normal as the next meal, something one went to as a matter of course. The saints were her familiars and would be invoked for their specialities – as Our Lady of Perpetual Succour in any mishap or calamity, St Anthony for something lost. Her spiritual life overflowed into generosity of all kinds; she was irrepressibly cheerful and sociable. Settled at Birch Lodge, the family home in Wimbledon, she slipped easily into English ways of domestic life: becoming a firm friend of a formidable cook, giving that implacable traditionalist lessons in Chilean specialities. She managed parlour- and house-maids, shared her life with nurses and governesses and a garrulous gardener. All this up to that other earthquake in her life: the outbreak of the Great War.

She came to live with me in her widowhood ten years later, away from Wimbledon, in a little house in Chelsea. She was a quiet loving companion in my turbulent twenties. One day the doctors advised her to have a little cyst in her spine removed to avoid, they said, probably crippled old age. I half-believe that she knew she might not survive the operation though it was not regarded as a critical one. As I waited outside the operating theatre of St Thomas's Hospital the surgeon, in tears, gave the news. There she lay, still warm and seemingly still strong. She is still vividly present to her four surviving children – now all in their eighties – with her courageous heart.

In most ways my father was a contrast to my mother. He was

austere and dedicated to his work, but widely appreciative of books and architecture. Cases of books came with him to England: Henry James, George Eliot, Conrad, Dickens ... and almost every political memoir of major importance was added to his library on publication. He had a large collection of French classics in a uniform binding of his choice. I doubt if there was any occasion, grave or trivial, to which he could not fit a quotation from Shakespeare. Hearing sisters in strident argument he would murmur to himself: 'Her voice was ever sweet, gentle and low – an excellent thing in a woman'; treading by mistake on a dog's mess in the street Keats would come to the rescue: 'I cannot see what flowers are at my feet'; chided by his eldest, somewhat caustic, daughter: 'How sharper than a serpent's tooth it is to have a thankless child.' There was no affectation in this. Thus spoke his humane and inclusive philosophy.

Having abandoned the kirk in his youth he grew in admiration of the Roman Catholic Church but without commitment to it until the last weeks of his life when he asked for a priest and the sacraments. His third son, by now a Jesuit priest, was there to minister to him.

I got to know him well from my ninth year, in the Great War. We played a lot of chess together and would pore over a large-scale map of the Western Front, moving little flags as it fluctuated. The personal agonies behind these little symbols were to be borne home later. My eldest brother, Charles, serving with the Field Artillery, was lightly wounded and invalided out to resume his medical studies. Next on the list was my eldest sister, Dorothy, swept from her prudish convent school to the full exposure of the crudity and many horrors of the big military hospital at Netley in Hampshire. The third child was David, an officer of the Black Watch, who combined the high qualities of both his parents and was, perhaps, their best beloved.

He was killed in Flanders, a few days short of his twentieth birthday and a couple of weeks short of the Armistice in 1918. An official telegram came late one evening to darkened Birch Lodge where I was alone with my mother. I dashed downstairs from my homework to know what it said. I did not need to read it. My mother was sitting in the hall, with the paper in her hands, looking into space, speechless. My father would be back soon from the City. I could not face their meeting so went back to my little room on the top floor. There, as I expected, I soon heard the clip-clopping of the four-wheeler which always met my father at the station, coming from the City. I heard him open the gate and walk down the drive, whistling as usual some wordless lament. After that there was silence for a long time.

There was no more plotting of the little flags on the map. Our war was over. Quite soon it was for everyone and they went mad with joy so that an awful irony was added to our empty world.

But suddenly the Spirit breathed on us and started something new. David's chaplain wrote to say he had been to Communion on the day before battle (we knew that he would if he could), and his captain and the adjutant of his regiment wrote with words of great sorrow, praise and affection. They eventually turned up at home, stayed on and became almost weekly visitors. And so it happened that David's adjutant, Tim Milroy, married my second sister, Clarita. He went from the army to the colonial service and spent his second lifetime as a district commissioner in Nigeria. They had one son, Dominic, who is a Benedictine monk and headmaster of Ampleforth.

David's body is buried in the little village of Slypscapelle in Belgium. After the war was over, my parents discovered his grave in the village churchyard, though David had been killed in Slyp Wood where he was given a hasty field burial. The villagers, in the wake of the Black Watch advance, had found the body with its 'R.C.' designation and had reburied it in their own churchyard, a rare thing to do. My father designed a gravestone and there it still stands with a great Celtic cross in granite at the head, the only grave in the churchyard, like a village memorial. The villagers held David's grave in special reverence and had tended it for over half a century. Years later, the local priest told my sister, Margaret, who was visiting the grave, that the village would like to have a ceremony to mark the seventieth

anniversary of David's death. It was an irresistible suggestion.
The family, including many younger relations, turned up in
force; the village was *en fete* with its band on parade. The Black
Watch sent an officer and piper in full rig to pay regimental
honours. The Mass was celebrated by my nephews, Dominic
Milroy and Mathew Burns (like Dominic, also of Ampleforth),
with the village priest. I said a few words at the graveside and the
national anthems of Belgium and Britain came nobly from the
village band. David's body was now surrounded by loving
people, not as it had been where he fell to a sniper's bullet in Slyp
Wood. Death was swallowed up in a little victory of the Spirit in
that family celebration.

I leave my father in quiet retirement, impoverished by the war
but enriched with many blessings. Tim Milroy had not only
married Clarita, but had introduced to us a younger brother, Bill,
who married my fourth sister, Alice, parents-to-be of a large
family. The Milroys thus became part of the Burns clan, and the
strong Scottish element balanced the Latinised family from Chile,
although the latter pulled its weight and both Milroys, sons of the
manse, came into the Church. My sister, Dorothy, married
another Scot: Jim Gordon, commander in the Royal Navy. An
English influence was brought to balance, with the marriage of
my third sister, Anita, to Basil John and my youngest sister,
Margaret, to Peter Whitfield. Both unions produced families of
talent and charm.

My parents seem to have settled into the English life as to the
manner born. The family's needs were always foremost. A house
was chosen within walking distance of the Jesuit college and the
Ursuline convent where we children were to be educated. That
part of Wimbledon where we lived has hardly changed in eighty
years. Our first house became a convent, but the garden is still
there and the grassy slopes which were mountains to me are now
gentle mounds. We spent a few years there and moved on to a

larger house, Birch Lodge, which became my boyhood world. I remember it mainly for its garden which was my wonderland. Beyond the terrace and the tennis-court there was a big rhododendron bush under which one could creep into a leafy darkness. A child treasures solitude – which so often makes him unhappy in later life. There was a sandpit where I made a trench and a dugout; a beech tree whose lower branches held a little hut. In such confinements my mind went free: I was soldier, spy, explorer, by choice.

My boyhood may be summed up in an 'Ode to T.F.B.' printed in the family magazine – *The B-Hive* – in 1916 when I was ten years old. My sister Clarita, who was fourteen at the time, was the author. To a later generation I should explain that Jack Johnson was the heavyweight boxing world champion, Sandow a weightlifter, Jimmy Wilde a flyweight boxing champion; the great comedian at the time, George Robey, often used the catchphrase quoted; Charlie, my eldest brother, was then a medical student engaged in dissection. Years later when I showed this poem to my Benedictine nephew, Dominic Milroy (aged 60), he exclaimed 'But you haven't changed at all!'

ODE TO T.F.B.

Tom is a funny little lad, you know –
He thinks that he's a boxer and as strong as Sandow.
He stands 4 feet in his socks about
But could beat Jack Johnson in a friendly bout.
'Meccano hasn't come' was his daily cry –
And it came and then what a mess – oh my!
Cranes and ships, aeroplanes by the score
Lie about all day on the nursery floor.
Then in they go into the cupboard of confiscation
And Tom sneaks them out again with great elation.
He's a connoisseur in chocolates is Thomas Ferrier
He smells them from afar like a sharp-nosed terrier.
He is a man of hobbies is T.F.B.
'I'm a dooced clever fellah!' he says with glee.

He's great on stamps and great at Soccer,
But at 'vulgar' jokes he's rather a shocker
He caricatures his family in the rudest way
He speculates with cunning and makes money every day.
Oh – he's great at finance – is Thomas B.
He'll be great at everything one day – you'll see.
What he'll be when he's a man remains to be seen
He'd make a great George Robey – 'the dooce he would old bean.'
But he'd rather be a General with a K.C.B.
With a V.C. thrown in, of course – but not an O.B.E.
He might be an inventor or a second Jimmy Wilde
A millionaire of course – but alone that's too mild.
But you did not know before that at chess he's a wonder
Of course he'll be World's Champion – he *never* makes a blunder
He beats Uncle John and Father into fits
With a pawn he knocks out Charlie who cuts people into bits
A broker, a boxer, a general, a comedian,
Latin Scholar, Chess Blue – but Tom is not a greedy 'un
Whatever career he follows, tho' – you bet your eye
Thomas Ferrier Burns will cause the dust to fly.

Wimbledon College was a private fee-paying Jesuit school of about 200 boys (it is now four times that size and state-aided). In the classic Jesuit tradition we progressed through grades with evocative names: Elements, Rudiments, Grammar, Syntax, Poetry and Rhetoric. Each class would be divided into Romans and Carthaginians, always in fierce competition to get marks from the master's questions. Each side had an 'imperator', a position much coveted for the privileges it earned. We were a happy lot of boys; the cliques and intolerances of public school were unknown to us. Most of us came from settled homes and often visited each other. We had very onerous homework but I founded a popular 'Last-minute Swat-Club' where work was parcelled out according to our gifts, so that one hopelessly indifferent in maths, for instance, would be helped out by one more expert, who in turn would be helped by a Latinist when he came to his own deficiency. Religion was taught by rote, by learning the Catechism by heart. Perhaps one had not done enough homework to know the seven gifts of the Holy Ghost or the various ways in which one shared in the guilt or sin of another. An inaccurate rendering of such lists could be sharply interrupted by the class-master – 'Catechism not known, Burns. Ask for six ferulas.' That was that. The ferula was like the sole of a long narrow shoe made of gutta percha. When brought down smartly on the open palm it stung like an electric shock but there was no lasting pain and we were spared the drudgery of writing lines. There was a special time for ferulas each day. One presented oneself to the master on duty and requested one's own punishment in a manner as detached as possible.

The mysteries of a faith have multitudinous ways of taking hold on consciousness. One was impressed from the start that the Christian religion is a historic and didactic one, implanted by teachers across the centuries. It did not begin and does not authentically continue with the inspiration, ideas or impositions of centuries later than the fourth, by which time it had got itself together, remembering and rendering into rules and dogmas the teaching of the Master.

I cannot recall having had any mental difficulty about the doctrine of the Real Presence. More privileged than most in this matter I was instructed at home by a good Jesuit, Fr Bearne. He brought to me, in a little silver box, a Communion wafer. It became, he explained, the Body and Blood of Jesus Christ at the words of the consecration in the Mass, when the priest repeated Christ's words at the Last Supper. I suppose that all Catholics undergo the same kind of mystification as did the apostles on that occasion. Here was a man, whose ways and words they barely understood, standing up and announcing that the bread in his hands was his body and that the wine he offered them to drink was his blood. This could have been no less mysterious in Jerusalem 2,000 years ago than in Wimbledon today.

The Jesuit gave me a little printed diagram which showed that there was not today a single minute round the clock when the words of consecration were not being repeated somewhere in the world. So it became for me just one more mode of God's

Chess in Chile, 1871. My maternal grandfather, Carlos Swinburne (right), with my mother standing behind him. His wife sits on his right and my mother's sisters and brother are grouped around my grandfather's chess opponent

Wimbledon, 1909. Myself, aged three, with my father

My mother (c. 1893)

London, 1986. Celebrating my 80th birthday with Mabél, our children and their husbands and wives: (standing, left) *Jonathan Parker with our daughter Maria-Belen (Burns) Parker; Carola (Nicodano) Burns with our son, David; Dolores (Luca de Tena) Burns with our son, Tom;* (sitting, at front) *Mary 'Kidge' (Addington) Burns and our son, Jimmy*

presence in the world. I was not more enlightened in later years by the learned treatises of theologians, like the Jesuit de la Taille or his Dominican opponent Garrigou-Lagrange. I doubt whether their immense exertions – not to mention those of the Scholastics – add anything to Eucharistic love, so palpable wherever the Eucharist is reserved in church or chapel: the subtlest greeting in an otherwise frigid and empty atmosphere.

Family Mass on Sundays, family feast-days, the building of a crib for Christmastide, the minor penances of Lent (no sweets!), the jubilation of Easter, with eggs hidden all over the garden; family plays, *The B-Hive* – with our drawings, stories and jokes (and I was just old enough, twelve years, to succeed my brother David as editor), tea dances, tennis parties . . . all served to fill the year's cycle and bind our family together and thus make life a sacral thing – a drawn-out ritual.

But that life died on 4 August 1914. We children were in a rented holiday house at Felixstowe at the time. I can remember the front page of the *Daily Mirror* on that day, wholly taken up with a photograph of the Kaiser with his waxed moustache and wearing the helmet of the Death's Head Hussars. Soldiers were already digging trenches in the green which overlooked the sea. We were packed up and brought home. There the war came nearer in the form of Belgian refugees who were temporarily settled in houses like ours, through our Catholic community. They were followed by groups of wounded soldiers from the local hospital in the bright blue flannel uniforms and red neckties adopted at that time. They came limping along, missing a limb perhaps, but infectiously cheerful, to play croquet in large tea-parties, shepherded by an urbane and ubiquitous Jesuit, Fr Martindale. I listened eagerly to their stories and became aware for the first time of 'abroad' and of battles there which – only for a brief time – spelt romance to me. It was only with my brother's death that I came to realise that many thousands of his kind – young and brave – had died before him, year after year, that these were of the best in the land, and that their deaths spelt the mutilation of a whole society. All this came to me as time went on and when the war poets told me more than the history books.

Meanwhile I spent 'a space of life between' in a self-contained family life, with its values untouched by the cataclysm.

2

A Jesuit Education

In my fourteenth year I went to Stonyhurst. How grateful I am to Wimbledon College and to my parents for keeping me at home instead of sending me away as a boarder to a prep school! There is probably no time in life when creature comforts, privacy with its hobbies and eccentricities, the pursuit and receipt of affection, is more treasured than in those years from, say, seven to twelve when the world is opening up and surprising us at every turn. To have all this institutionalised and regulated by and with strangers may be 'character-forming', but in these circumstances the character is being formed before it is half created. Home and family life is the most effective catalyst for drawing a boy's inchoate desires and experiences together.

I came to Stonyhurst to find a civilised society already in being. There was no bullying. Of course, cliques and snobberies abounded but there was a wide variety of friends to choose from. This was especially true of Stonyhurst which is not divided in a perpendicular fashion into houses of thirty or so, with older boys and much younger ones living all together. The school was divided by 'playrooms', according to age groups. Each playroom was a world on its own with perhaps more than 100 boys of one's own age, with its own recreation room and playground, its own sports teams and so on, and its own 'playroom master', who was supposed to be specially suited to deal with the age group in his charge. He was not a sort of father-figure to a family of all ages, as with house-masters.

A public school is inevitably a homosexual society but this segregation by age, apart from the general ethos of the place, gave little opportunity for what used to be called 'unnatural vice'. There were *amitiés amoureuses* indeed and these were part of life, idealising rather than idolising one's object of affection. We called it 'tarting' and few took it very seriously.

Religion was really the binding element in the school. Our year would start with a three-day 'retreat'. This meant there were regular 'meditations' or talks by the retreat-master (each playroom had its own, geared to its stage of maturity) on the mysteries of the faith or moral problems. There was plenty of free time but no games. Silence was obligatory throughout the day in the whole school. Reading was confined to saints' lives and the like. The rule was liberally interpreted. Chesterton's Father Brown stories were legitimate. This retreat was, of course, a godsend for a new boy who had his chance to get the geography of the enormous place clear in his head, to observe his fellows unmolested, to have an undemanding schedule plus the bonus of some spiritual encouragement. There was nothing Jansenistic about the 'Jays' as we always called our teachers.

It was a good settling-down period after the long vac and before the strenuous routine took over. The retreat-givers were not on the staff but visitors, and one was free to raise with them any problems, including those which would be difficult to discuss with those actually in charge of our daily lives. Every morning Mass was obligatory as well as night prayers in the school chapel. That none of this was particularly onerous or strange may be seen in the fact that it was quite normal for boys to pop into the chapel at any odd moment of their own free will.

We were very far from being a sanctimonious lot despite these disciplines: simply, religion had a central place in daily life and gave it a sort of amplitude and ease of mind which would be atrophied in a purely secular flat-earth regime. I would say that for a general education Stonyhurst College could hardly be bettered. A great deal was left to personal initiative in the various voluntary clubs, in the debating society, in plays or concerts and in elocution competitions. Its actual teaching was generally poor. The staff were Jesuits at different stages of their training, they had not joined up to be schoolteachers; the Jesuit vocation is missionary in the widest sense. I understand that the school today is entirely staffed by professional lay-masters right up to the Head. This presumably has greatly improved standards for the examinee material which schoolboys have become. But something must be missing now when those men in black have all disappeared, leaving one old priest or two to attend to spiritual needs. The idea that there is a Jesuit 'type' is laughable to anyone who has lived with dozens and found them all different. A very few were unpleasant, nearly all were kindly, mortified men of widely differing backgrounds and achievements.

The biggest bonus that a public school has to offer is in being a field where friendships may spring up, like aconites, in unexpected places. My own experience of this was immediate. As soon as I boarded the crowded school train at Euston I was repulsed from one carriage to another with cries of, 'No room, no room.' I made my way to the last carriage. Here, four ill-assorted boys were wedged into the corner seats but grudgingly admitted that there was room for me. I sensed that they were all unpopular and disliked each other. I sat next to one, deep in a book, who had hardly stirred. He was my age, he had gypsy good looks, with a certain air of nobility. I soon discovered that he was reading Chesterton's *Orthodoxy*. I happened to be reading his *Heretics*. It was a conclusive coincidence. I had found a mind and temperament very different but totally congruent with my own. Perhaps I became Doctor Watson to his Sherlock Holmes, as he was a genius and always the innovator, but we made a redoubtable pair as time went on.

The school train finally stopped at Whalley, near Blackburn, where buses awaited us to take us for the next few miles. It was pandemonium in the dark with much pushing and scrambling for places. My new friend said: 'There's no hurry, we can get on later. There's a good pub across the road.' Once installed there he asked in an off-hand way: 'Do you like port?' I said yes without knowing anything about the stuff. We each had generous beakers and managed to slip easily into the last bus, warm inside and out.

I soon saw that he was as old-timer at the school and a loner, detached from his fellows. He turned out to be Henry John, one of the great progeny of Augustus, who had been adopted by an aunt when his mother had died in his infancy. The aunt – the mother's sister – had become a Catholic and had sent this rather wild cuckoo in her nest to the care of the Jesuits. Their sagacious and tolerant discipline certainly steered a development of mind and character which might so easily have been dissipated. After my first year we were promoted to rooms and found two at the far end of an old wing, called 'Shirk' with good reason. Inter-room visiting was forbidden but was constant. To be sure we were in our right places by the time he checked up on us, the Jay in charge of the wing would call out, 'I'm coming up,' as he approached and thus was sure of finding everything in order when he arrived on his infrequent visits. That was enlightened discipline.

In 1923, Fr Martin D'Arcy was appointed to the staff and so began a friendship between us that was to last until his death in 1976. His appointment, as he has recounted in his *Laughter and the Love of Friends* (1991), was especially to keep an eye on Henry and me.

Schoolwork – and prizes – came easily to the two of us; we forged neck and neck into wider horizons. We were omnivorous readers. Henry, on a holiday trip to Paris, had smuggled back a first edition of *Ulysses*, at that time banned by HM Customs. We would discuss it at length with Fr D'Arcy. He also introduced us to the poetry of Gerard Manley Hopkins – virtually unknown at the time – and to Baron von Hügel, a leading Modernist and mystical theologian. I still treasure the Baron's great two-volume classic, *The Mystical Element in Religion*, inscribed to me by Henry and two other friends on my seventeeth birthday.

My wife, when I took her to see Stonyhurst years later, was amazed to see a man covered with mud and shouting instructions as a rugger coach, later half-naked in the swimming bath, and later still officiating with great dignity, resplendent in a cope, at Solemn Benediction amid clouds of incense and the well-known full-bellied roar of our hymn-singing. It was a far cry from the notorious novel of the 1920s, *A.M.D.G.*, about a Spanish Jesuit school by our family friend Ramon Perez de Ayala, ambassador in London at the time of the Republic; a far cry too from James Joyce's *Portrait of the Artist as a Young Man*.

Stonyhurst was *sui generis*, with a history beginning in exile under the Elizabethan persecution, the first boys coming in secret to a recusant gentleman's home in Lancashire. Gradually added to it in the nineteenth century was a vast building which could house nearly 1,000 under one roof. It had a barrack-like quality, and indeed something of a military spirit pervades it. We had portraits of our many VCs looking down on us in the refectory. The Officers Training Corps was quite popular, with its band, parades and annual inter-school camps. A sergeant-major from Sandhurst bawled us into martial order. I eventually became a martinet myself with a crown on my sleeve, a stick under my arm and a powerful voice of command.

Henry stayed in the ranks, a hopeless bungler at drill but enterprising on field days. He would have made a good *maquisard*. He had an adventurous, not to say reckless, spirit just below the surface. It showed itself in climbing out of the building in the dead of night and in, to me, sickening exploits in tree-climbing. Most of all, this came to the fore in Henry's favourite method of long-distance transport, by what he called 'lorry-hopping' which involved jumping on to the backs of lorries going in our direction, maybe from London to his father's home in Hampshire. In our *argot* there were either 'hairy bums' or 'lousy bums' according to whether they provided foot and hand hold at the rear or none. I found it exhilarating and terrifying to travel this way but now often wonder how we survived. I was by instinct physically timid, Henry the reverse. Our *attraits* and achievements differed in many other ways. He was girl-shy in a way that I was not. Though he longed to excel in the art, he was a very *gauche* dancer despite the efforts of his beguiling young half-sisters, Poppet and Vyvian, in the holidays.

I was in many ways more conventional than Henry, but intellectually we saw eye-to-eye. We were not as yet politicised but we hated the ruling culture, seeing it as secularist, self-seeking and self-sufficient. In religion we could not tolerate indifferentism. We were too polemical to be priggish. Catholic doctrine and its defence as taught in the upper forms bored us and everybody else. We suggested a revolutionary change which was accepted and worked marvels for a time. It consisted in taking the religious doctrine class out into the playground. Here, half-a-dozen boys would mount soap-boxes as at Speakers' Corner in Hyde Park and expound some particular aspect of Catholic doctrine as if to an infidel crowd. The crowd was allowed to heckle and argue from an heretical or other point of view; the speaker had to be prepared with his answers. The proceedings were uproarious but amazingly instructive. I was invited over to Ampleforth by Fr Paul Nevill, a great headmaster of the time, to explain the whole idea, but my effort fell flat. Combat was apparently not the keynote of the Benedictine spirit – which I have since grown to respect so much.

Schooldays came to an end. It had been a world in microcosm with its layers of experience, its loves and hates, its loneliness, its drudgery and excitements. The pitch and tone of life there tended to make us, for a time, strangers in the larger world; but at least we came to it not without arms or armour and with a sense of independence and purpose.

My little band of friends dispersed. Henry had already decided to join the Jesuits; I resisted some pressures since all my inclinations were for a life where women would be inevitable and integral to it. Henry was too young to join the Society immediately; Fr D'Arcy arranged for him to go to Rome and lodge in the Beda College and attend lectures at the Jesuit university there, the Gregoriana. The Beda was a foundation primarily for convert clergymen who wanted or needed a simplified course in theology before being conditionally ordained into the Roman priesthood. It also housed a few more or less eccentric laymen and was presided over by Mgr Duchemin, one of the wisest priests and administrators that I have met. He was himself a convert clergyman and knew the hang-ups, fears and hopes of his variegated flock and he was a marvellous host.

Henry became absorbed in a side of Roman life unknown to anyone save professional theologians: the Schools. Here, the crowded halls would resound to lectures in Latin on theology and philosophy as they had ever since the Middle Ages. There was no bleak uniformity but contrasting views, some of them almost revolutionary as had been the teaching of Thomas Aquinas and the revival of Aristotelian philosophy. Henry was never one for half-measures and became absorbed, putting his health at risk in the heady atmosphere. After two terms he needed a complete change and took it with me in a somewhat fantastic exploration in Tripoli and Tunisia. His idea was to search out the troglodytes who lived under the earth and if possible Ouled Nails, belly dancers of legendary sensuality.

He had it all worked out except the details. From Palermo we took a ship which offered steerage or deck passage. The latter was preferable as the large communal cabin was filled with Arabs. The atmosphere was fetid and resonant with the snores, belches and farts of the recumbent inmates who apparently never emerged on deck. We would lift a hatch now and then to savour the sound and smells and drop it, overtaken with a sort of laughing gas. There were two meals of pasta a day from the cook's galley. From Tripoli we took a train towards Togourt. The third class had no seats and with our Arab companions we squatted on the floor, sharing their sparse and scented food cooked on the spot and drinking from their earthenware water-jugs. There were various halts when the travellers could descend and relieve themselves in the sand or else walk off to the horizon.

So gradually we proceeded to our destination. At one point a couple of German zoologists who, they said, were scanning the desert for some rare fauna for the Berlin zoo, picked us up in their large car and put us well on our way.

Three days and nights by camel were a specially memorable part of the journey. Our guide could only say *couscous*, which we took to mean to halt and share a greasy concoction of his, helped out by dates. We were always hungry and happily his date supply was strapped to the back of his camel in an open-work bag. It was possible to sidle up and grab a sticky handful as he nodded in his saddle. Once a sandstorm erupted and cut us off from sight and sounds. Momentarily I despaired of ever seeing Henry or the guide again. I said a prayer in that pitiless place and dropped the reins, letting the camel find its own way. It did. When the storm blew over we were within a few yards of each other.

The troglodytes were at last discovered and it was no disappointment. There they were in countless caves dug into the sides of vast craters, but alas I cannot recall any meeting with Ouled Nails.

Our night stops were in the native *fonduks* which for sheer squalor could hardly be bettered anywhere in the world. A large quadrangle made of bare single-storey cells – most clients carried their bedding with them – served as the stabling of camels and mules. Men and animals were all locked in at an early hour. There we were without light or water save what we brought with us. With a flashlight – or indeed without one – it was obvious that the cell was infested with vermin. Sitting on hard chairs – the only furniture – was the only way of keeping them at bay. In other cells little oil lamps would burn and there would be the whiff of cooking and a grumbling murmur of talk.

At first light the muleteers and camel drovers were prodding and kicking their beasts into action, tightening their girths and heaving heavy saddles and loads into place. The great gates opened and the caravan moved on, the dust shining in the first shafts of sunlight. Not all *fonduks* are beyond redemption in their squalor. It is better if they have no paddock or camels attached. In one of the better sort Henry had a high fever and what looked to me like dysentery. I found some coarse biscuits and something like rum in the village. He recovered after a few days of this treatment.

In the ruins of Carthage was a triumphant finale: shades and phrases of Augustine came from the stones and we exulted in a journey accomplished and the majestic remains of a civilisation.

We kept on our native dress as far as London. In the Dover-London train we discouraged any invasion of our railway carriage by shouting at each other in imaginary Arabic and with wild gesticulations. Henry suggested we go straight to the Jesuit headquarters in Farm Street where we greatly embarrassed a bewildered Fr D'Arcy. It was the parting of the ways: Henry went to the Jesuit novitiate at Manresa House in Roehampton, there to begin the first stage of thirteen years' training for the priesthood.

At that time the noviceship seemed to reduce its young men to pious zombies, shunning any spark of worldliness, suppressed and over-scrupulous. For Henry there was much spiritual and sexual torment as I came to know later. He survived a period of study before going to Campion Hall, the Jesuit house at Oxford. Sporadic periods of hectic gaiety and deep gloom distanced him from me when we might occasionally meet. I was not surprised when he left the Jesuits.

For him there followed a period of what could be called 'busily seeking in continual change' and close encounters with girls, some of them my friends, encounters which were too often disconcerting on both sides. When he was killed cliff-climbing in Cornwall, suicide was suggested. But to me that was totally out of the question: he was a lover of life if ever there was one, but from his schooldays he had been madly reckless. His beloved dog was found sitting by Henry's clothes at the cliff-top. He had meant to get back. His body was found at sea days later. As Augustus wrote with what seemed to me obscene callousness, 'it had apparently suffered the attention of sea-gulls'. But Augustus was good enough to ask Fr D'Arcy to say a requiem Mass and I went down with some of the John family for the burial. Neither Augustus nor anyone there could quench their grief. Henry had given much more than joy to my youth, but his last years had disclosed a chasm between us and had filled me with foreboding.

3
A Student in Paris

Leaving Stonyhurst, I went to Paris in 1924 with an open mind and a small purse. The prospect of Oxbridge had not attracted me: it would mean a financial strain on my parents and a postponement of the wider world which I wanted to meet.

My first encounter with the city was not encouraging. I lodged with a solidly bourgeois family near the Eiffel Tower. It catered for students with plain living and something less than high thinking. It was a teetotal *ménage* and I soon disgraced myself by smuggling in a bottle of wine. In the bitter cold of my little bedroom I plunged it into the jug of hot water provided each evening before dinner. The freezing bottle cracked and the vinous fumes enveloped the gloomy landing to the evident disapproval of *monsieur* and *madame*. I decided to move out on my own and rented a room in a sleazy hotel in Montparnasse, just round the corner from the *boulevard* and the Café de la Coupole. A marble table became my student's desk. There a coffee and a croissant would entitle me to pass the morning undisturbed. The *quoi écrire* could be requested as a matter of course from the obliging *garçon*.

It was not quite the Paris that I had been reading about, which had cast a spell on Henry and myself in our last year at school, when final exams were over: Paris of the *fin-de-siècle*. We saw life in dramatic terms and the admixture of satanism and sanctity to be found in Baudelaire and Rimbaud fascinated us with its anarchic mysticism. Two novelists also caught our fancy: Joris-Karl Huysmans and Léon Bloy. The first wrote a series of semi-autobiographical novels, verging on prolixity, about the scabrous depravity of his earlier life, with such titles as *A Rebours* and *Là-bas*. They would have been pointless had they not led to his conversion and the evocation of Chartres in his incomparable semi-novel, *La Cathédrale*. We found his involuted symbolism hilarious. He was a living exaggeration of his own epoch. Léon Bloy was totally different: his *oeuvre* is, in effect, a second book of Job. He lived in abject poverty, he roared against contemporary atheism in journals and novels: a veritable prophet. I did not know until later that, under God, he had converted Jacques Maritain and his wife, who were to be my mainstay in Paris. What all these men had in common was a search for the Absolute. I did not expect to get dusty answers in Paris and I was not disappointed. There was nothing *fin-de-siècle* about my discoveries, but the springtime of a Catholic revival, a resurrection from the killing-fields of Flanders.

Shakespeare and Company, run by friendly and sagacious Sylvia Beach, published the first edition of Joyce's *Ulysses*: it was the meeting-place for aspirant American writers immersing themselves in bohemian life after their war experiences or as an escape from their native land. It must have been there that I met James Joyce's wife, a big-hearted Irish woman who enveloped me and took me to the Joyce home. The master was away but for me there was the imagined effulgence of his spirit and there was also a warm welcome from Joyce's son who looked like Yeats in his youth. He was taking a singing course at the Conservatoire.

I was in search of some sort of integration. Suddenly what looked like a key to this came into my hands: a book by Jacques Maritain. He was then a by-word on the Left Bank and beyond, the prophet of neo-Thomism. It was a world of philosophy just faintly familiar to me. Eric Gill had put me on to Maritain's *Philosophy of Art*, a little book printed at Ditchling, but here at hand was a whole *opus*, an invasion of all my chosen fields of thought. I can't remember now which of Maritain's many books I picked up at my favourite bookshop and took to a sunny bench in the Luxembourg Gardens, but it is immaterial as the *leitmotif* was always the same. I found it telling me what I wanted to know. New knowledge is mostly a matter of recognition, as is the first meeting of friends or lovers. Searching is impelled by some spirit within us, for something obscured but already found. 'Be comforted. You would not be seeking Me if you had not found Me,' Jesus said to Pascal, as I was to read much later.

The sun set on the Luxembourg Gardens and I repaired to La Coupole. I presume that I ordered a pernod *à l'eau* to steady myself from this eye-opener. I wrote to Maritain trying to explain myself and asking to see him. Back came a letter inviting me to his home in Meudon, a subdued suburb, for the following Sunday.

I was greeted by a short stooping figure with his head on one side, as if listening to music. A shock of dark hair over an incandescent face, with a smile that went up to his eyes. A snatch of Hopkins came into my head: 'I came into a house where all were good to me, God knows deserving no such thing.'

Welcomed by all, I was finally seated in a circle which gradually came into focus. There was Raïssa, his beautiful Jewish-Russian wife whose dark eyes seemed to be searching spaces beyond my reach but suddenly bearing down on Gwen John, a mousy little woman shrinking into herself with shyness. There too was Raïssa's buxom sister and a rangy young man with eyes askew. He turned out to be Emmanuel Mounier, editor of *Esprit*, an *avant-garde* left-wing Catholic monthly. I suppose Gabriel Marcel was there, otherwise I can't see how I could have come to know him. He was a dramatist, a personalist philosopher, a poet and a talented pianist, as it later turned out. He would weep gently as he played Bach in his studio and weep at Mass in the Benedictine convent in the Rue du Bac, but one could also rejoice with him in his incessant conversation: I came to respect his gift of tears, seeing it as an acknowledgement of inadequacy before the Absolute. I have always had it to some extent, though I admit that the bagpipes affect me just as much as a Gospel passage.

I felt at first like a fleshy bull in a spiritual china shop but was gradually made to feel at home. Through that gathering, often repeated, Paris became to me a new world.

Maritain's intimate circle consisted for the most part of the writers of a series of books called *Le Roseau d'Or*. They varied in subject from fiction to philosophy but were united in a new-found hope and confidence which was the keynote of the Catholic revival, so catholic also in its range of appreciation. There was nothing clerical nor particularly conformist in the work of Stanislaus Fumet, Henri Ghéon, Julien Green or René Schwob, but the anchor-man was Maritain.

Some were tempted by, but did not fall for, the strident calls of the Action Française, on the extreme right wing of politics. And there was a certain rigorism in the integrated, if not integralist theology propounded by Maritain and his Dominican mentors like Clerrisac and Garrigou-Lagrange. St Thomas Aquinas had all the answers, it seemed. I wasn't quite so sure.

Through desultory reading I stumbled on Maine de Biran's *Journal Intime* which seems to me a classic of introspection; the work of a man finding God through a relentless search for his identity. Then the volcanic mountain of Maurice Blondel's *Action* came into view, and Laberthonnière, whose writing seemed to bear down on what was, to me, the basic question – the problem of ourselves. What are we and what ought we to be? Any thinking which avoided this question seemed to me so much sophistry.

The fashionable philosophers of the time, who so often made an awful muddle of their own lives, became irrelevant. One had to go deeper, to the deep-sea life of the spiritual writers such as Gratry and de Caussade. Here was familiarity with the suburbs of eternity. The presence of God was their environment, where they were confidently at home.

It became clear that religious controversy, as popularly expounded, was in reality a surface disturbance. The scintillating mackerel-catches of one intellectual or another did not affect or disturb the ocean depths. At this point the mind may boggle or dispute or else be conscious of infinite mystery and indeed be part of it – not separated as one is from a problem outside oneself.

I would never denigrate the work of scalpel and hatchet of a Maritain and the neo-Thomists. They were doing a fine job in clarifying and castigating much muddled agnosticism and the evasions of its prophets. But the reassurance of the great French spiritual masters moved in. I recognised the human condition which they took for granted with such tenderness. The immanence and immediacy of God, which they taught me as a matter of fact, came to be quietly convincing.

My little room in the Rue Bréa, my café table, my wandering and wondering in every corner of Paris, gave me no slick solutions, but much solace and strength: what I was looking for.

I should add that my life was not, after all, only a segregated swatting on book after book. Human encounters came like ministering angels. Maritain gave me a note to Chagall and that wonderfully kind and mystical Russian Jew made me at home in his studio, all alight with his painting and panels of stained glass. Of Gwen John it is difficult to speak. At the time I knew nothing of her passionate love affair with Rodin, nor her equally passionate love for Maritain's sister-in-law. We had a bond in Henry, her nephew and my best friend in those days. We talked, in her seclusion, of our common faith. She would send little notes in a sort of schoolgirl handwriting and vocabulary. I never suspected spent passions or I might have felt more at ease with her.

After months without measure, so packed were they with impressions and discoveries, I concluded that I must go home and earn my living. I had undergone a sort of implosion with effects that have never left me. With the exception of occasional lectures at the Sorbonne and the Institute Catholique, I had bypassed formal academic life. Reading now my friends' memoirs of their Oxford days, I wonder if I missed very much. Certainly there were big gaps in my knowledge; I had missed some donnish sophistries as well as my friends' high jinks and light-hearted or sentimental debaucheries, but I had no regrets. In any case we evened out in later life. Frank Longford once remarked in surprise when I told him I had skipped university: 'But I always thought you had been to Oxford *and* Cambridge.' Michael Trappes-Lomax, by then installed as Rouge Dragon at the College of Heralds, said with his inimitable stutter: 'At any rate you were never b-b-buggered by a dreaming spire.' Perhaps I had acquired some kinship with the wandering scholars who drifted in the thirteenth century to Paris or Bologna. Sometimes the words of Christopher Smart come back to me: 'For in my nature I quested for beauty, but God, God hath sent me to sea for pearls.'

It surprises me now that I had no urge for sex during all my time in Paris. Things are not explained simply by putting them into words. To say that I 'sublimated' my 'libido' simply relates one enigma to another. The fact is that only commercialised sex was on offer and this happens to disenchant me.

4
First Steps in Publishing

The transition from Paris to London in 1925 and a job in the City could not have been more abrupt and complete. Everything, from the whiff of the Metro, the scents of black tobacco and strong coffee, the wheezing of accordions in a *bal musette*, the lure of the Left-Bank bookshops, the exciting journey through the jungle of philosophy, poetry and painting in the Paris of those days, the tentative penetration to one's own essential solitude – all this receded before the impact of a totally different way of living.

I found myself suddenly at a desk in the City, in an import and export business connected with South America and Chile in particular. I was dealing with technical terms which might have been in Sanskrit for all I understood. I was supervised by stuffy self-important managers in an ill-lit asylum of glass partitions effectively excluding even the drab little human contacts one might have expected. The long trek from Wimbledon to Waterloo, and by tube to the City, crushed by fellow-travellers in the rush-hours of morning and evening, was made the more miserable by confronting what I took to be blank resignation or else smug satisfaction in the faces of my fellow travellers. Now, much later, living near Victoria Station, I have come to admire the patience of the commuter, enduring packed rush-hour buses and underground, to and from suburbia with its little gardens and confrontations with wife and family, and a mortgage.

To come home at evening was to reach an oasis. Here I could go back to my Paris books: my beloved Maritain was at my elbow; a two-volume work on comparative religion by a Jesuit, Pinard de la Boullaye, opened my eyes to the distant Himalayas of the eastern religions; the existentialism of Gabriel Marcel, no less than the essentially messianic ruminations of a Soloviev or a Berdyaev, kept me on the alert against rigidities of dogmatism. To me, then, the religious experience was as variegated with light and shade and colour as if it were a vast landscape glimpsed through passing clouds from a mountain top, and I simply could not understand the apathy of most people towards such a many-splendoured thing. I learnt how to keep it dark and hidden in my consciousness: *secretum meum mihi* was the watchword.

Soon after getting back to London I rejoined the Catholic Evidence Guild (CEG). The lessons I had learnt in the Stonyhurst playground were now for real. There were classes to be followed on an occasional evening, handouts to be studied on almost everything from holiness to hell. There were few difficulties and no mysteries about the faith for the CEG: our arguments were cut and dried and certainly convinced ourselves if nobody else. We were an odd lot, from barristers and bank clerks to a remarkable charlady who reputedly had read the whole of the *Summa* of Thomas Aquinas and could trot out Aristotelian concepts in her Clapham cockney as easy as pie. As I went on speaking assignments anywhere from Speaker's Corner in Hyde Park to the Round Pond on Hampstead Heath, and street corners in places such as Harlesden which I had never heard of, it was like being a secret agent in a foreign land, with a mixture of excitement and dread of self-betrayal. The pick-up point for a platform (little more than a step-ladder) had been indicated – perhaps a little newsagent in a drab back-street – and it would also be the meeting point for my companion-conspirator, man or woman, and we were off on our own. One talked to be heckled, so as to draw a crowd. Not a few of the hecklers were professionals from the Protestant Alliance or the Rationalist Association. One came to know them and anticipate the questions which they shouted at us. With their bowler hats and mackintoshes and loud rasping voices, I imagined them as KGB men.

The soap-box became part of my weekend world. Sometimes

one prayed for rain, so as to be let off the job. But, again, it would be bliss when it was done, sharing strong tea and doorstep sandwiches with one's mate for that evening, swapping impressions in some local café. I was careful to hide these missions from my friends in my other world, that of cocktail parties and nightclubs, careful never to arouse suspicions of being devout or different in any way. Righteousness and self-satisfaction were temptations to be resisted, more sinister and soul-destroying than sexual desire.

In the end I found the street-corner level of controversy tedious, and the strain of a double life too hard to bear. So I left the guild as suddenly as I had leapt into it. But by that time (1926) Frank Sheed, the master of the CEG, had invited me to join him in a Catholic publishing enterprise which he was about to launch. It was a chance of escaping from the City. Publishing, like diplomacy, would be conducting my proselytising warfare by other means. So with unaffected joy I found myself stepping down from one sort of soap-box and sitting on another in the then makeshift offices of Sheed & Ward. (Frank's wife, Maisie Ward, was the other half of the partnership.)

I was not unprepared for the trade. From my schooldays it had been in mind. I had a reverence for a great-uncle, James Burns, an Anglican publisher who had followed his friend John Henry Newman into the Catholic fold. He lost his livelihood as a result, but with the help of Newman's gift of the copyright of *Loss and Gain* and other works, gradually restored it under the imprint of Burns & Oates. There was no family succession because his only son became a priest (and died while preaching in the Brompton Oratory) and his five daughters became Ursuline nuns. I remember, at the age of four or so, bumping on my bottom from the top of their convent's waxed stairway and being comforted with the sort of cakes that only nuns seem to concoct. It was a comforting if not a comfortable connection with the founder's family.

Some day perhaps, I would think, the Burns family might be in business again. In my teenage Burns & Oates was a well-established imprint and known throughout the English-speaking Catholic world.

At that time I would nourish myself on books like Stanley Unwin's methodical treatise on the book trade. Lettering and typography fascinated me and the magic names of Bell, Baskerville, Bodoni and Bembo were typefaces familiar to me. I knew how to reckon the reams of paper required for any quantity of books and any book as such had its fascination and even, it seemed, its radioactive quality. If I had some theoretical preparation for the job, I had as little practical knowledge of it as my employer.

Frank Sheed was a wiry Australian barrister with a head too big for his body, scant hair, deep-set small eyes, and a bottle-nose (though he was a teetotaller). A wide grin intercepted almost every sentence in his staccato talk. He had a daunting repertoire of music-hall songs and jokes plus a wealth of clerical gossip, in sharp contrast to his platform *persona*. I owe him so much for the trust that he put in me, for his enthusiasm for any plan or project that occurred to me, for giving me self-confidence, that any note of criticism or antipathy would here be out of place. Sheed & Ward was a sweat-shop and a university rolled into one.

The first excitement in the office was the publication of Hilaire Belloc's *A Companion to H. G. Wells' Outline of History* in 1926. Wells was very much in vogue at the time and *Outline of History* was his secularist prophecy. Belloc's *Companion* was sharply personal in tone: Wells was uneducated, insular, ignorant of foreign languages, lower middle class and untrustworthy. Wells replied with a witty pamphlet, *Mr Belloc Objects*, where he suggested that Mr Belloc had apparently been born all over Europe. Belloc came up fighting in the third round, *Mr Belloc Still Objects*. The whole affair launched Sheed & Ward into the limelight.

Belloc had been one of the heroes of my schooldays, and *The Path to Rome*, written in 1902 when he was thirty-one, a call to adventure. He had been exceedingly courteous to an unknown gangling teenager who had gone to him for advice as to how to cross the Pyrenees on foot (of which more anon), and here he was in my little office, bustling in with his great black cloak. 'May I use your telephone?' was usually his first question, and there followed seemingly endless calls to evening hostesses, errant children, editors, to all and sundry, before we got down to business. Editing his *Essays of a Catholic* (1931), I asked him for the origin of a quotation on the title page, 'Truth comes by conflict.' Was it perhaps Tertullian? I tentatively enquired. 'No, I wrote it myself. Let it stand.'

There was always a sense of urgency in our meetings and they were hard to come by. I remember telephoning him at his office in Baker Street where he would seclude himself to dictate to his long-suffering secretary 'Bunny' Soames. Could he conceivably come by for an urgent consultation? I asked. He answered, 'I am pressed for time but we could meet somewhere midway between Baker Street and the Reform Club where I shall be dining.' (In this and subsequent passages readers should add several guttural Rs wherever the letter occurs to get some flavour of his unique accent.)

In a moment of inspiration I suggested the Café Royal. 'Excellent. I shall be with you at six o' clock.' So over the marble tables and lager, at that time an admirable feature of the establishment, we did our business. He looked suddenly reflective. 'Lager should be accompanied by oysters. Let us repair to Bentley's.' That delectable bar was almost across the road and we ate a dozen with relish and light talk. 'Oysters are the preliminary to a good dinner. Let us go to the Escargot Bienvenu.' Wonderingly I followed him into darkest Soho. Belloc was received with the reverence that surrounds the visit of a papal nuncio to a local parish church. We had a splendid meal and, emboldened by the wine, I ventured on personal matters, asking what could be done about what the catechism roundly calls 'the lusts of the flesh', by which, indeed, I was much afflicted at the time. 'My dear boy, the Catholic Church says *you must not roger* – and that is the fact of the matter.' The harsh teaching seemed temporally acceptable in such an atmosphere. Eventually I lifted him home to South Kensington in a taxi. He had forgotten about the Reform Club; I had something to remember all my days. My children's generation know almost nothing of Belloc. But he was endearing to those who were close to him and will be enduring for his poetry where something of a great soul may be discerned, and for his very funny verses for children of all ages.

Chesterton was another founding father of the firm with a slim book of verses, *Our Lady of the Seven Swords*, and later a book of essays. He gave us what he could spare, but was mostly committed elsewhere by previous contracts. G.K. was by nature gregarious but was kept by his wife in some isolation at their house in Beaconsfield. The ritual drinking sessions of the Chesterbellocians might otherwise have been his undoing.

Odd how an isolated incident often lodges a person in one's memory rather than a general impression. Thus I remember one morning bowling down Whitehall in a taxi with G.K. As we approached the Cenotaph he suddenly cut off his chatter and, in silence, swept his big black hat from his head as we passed it. Few men perform such sacramentals in the privacy that a taxi provides.

He had been my idol in my schooldays and has survived every cross-current in my thought for sixty years. His writing, as light and dexterous and timeless as a coracle, still rides the tide, the swell and the storm of human cogitation and behaviour.

Ronald Knox had published his *apologia, A Spiritual Aeneid*, in 1918. Sheed & Ward soon re-issued it with a new preface. This was followed by volumes of sermons and conferences interspersed with such *tours de force* as *Essays in Satire* (1928) and *Broadcast Minds* (1932). Meanwhile, with another publisher, Knox produced a steady stream of detective stories by which he mainly financed his Oxford chaplaincy from 1926 to 1939.

It was there that I used to see him on Sheed & Ward business.

*Henry John. Portrait
(c. 1923) by his father,
Augustus John*

*Fr Martin D'Arcy.
Portrait (c. 1940) by
Augustus John*

Early influences: (from top, clockwise)
Jacques Maritain; Fr Ronald Knox; G. K.
Chesterton; Hilaire Belloc

Ronnie, as almost everyone called him, was a self-effacing character, apparently lethargic and diffident. But he had a bubbling, wry sense of humour in him which often surfaced with grunts and a heaving of his shoulders at his own sallies. I remember him mostly squatting on his club-fender in his study at the chaplaincy, pulling at an interminable pipe. His front door was open to all comers and his time seemed to be always at their disposal.

For all that his output was immense and apparently effortless, he had none of the quirks or affectations of most writers; certainly none of the vanity of a man who had carried off all the prizes at Oxford as an undergraduate, nothing of the donnish characteristics of those who spent the greater part of their lives in the secluded, all-male, rarefied atmosphere of the university at that period.

There could hardly have been a stronger contrast between two ex-Anglican divines than that of Ronald Knox with Vernon Johnson whose own *apologia*, *One Lord, One Faith*, Sheed & Ward published in 1929. 'Father Vernon' had been a spellbinder at Anglo-Catholic conferences. Eloquent, sentimental, unsophisticated and devout, he was as solidly set in the English scene as any country parish church. Clearly it had been immensely costing to enter a different atmosphere. I remember his haggard face, his anxious, almost timid questions, as we met to discuss the publication of his book. His going over to Rome had been a well-kept secret. His main concern was not to hurt the host of his Anglican friends, and to explain his move in terms which they could understand. His little book made no pretension to scholarship. It was his personal schism with the Church which he wanted to sew up for himself, in the simplest way. There was surely something lacking in the Catholic structure and leadership at the time when it could hardly offer an appropriate place and function for such a man as Vernon Johnson. He made both his own, in the end, in comparative obscurity, preaching the 'little way' of St Theresa of Lisieux and practising what he preached.

Yet another contrasting character in those early days and

thereafter was Arnold Lunn. Reading between the lines of an earlier book, *Roman Converts* (1924), which discussed Chesterton, Ronald Knox and others, it struck me that the book was rather an apologia for those that he criticised than a refutation of their views. It was no surprise to me when he joined a band which he couldn't beat. Ronald Knox received him into the Church in 1933.

Lunn was a tempestuous but ever-welcome intruder at the office. He dished up books of theology and apologetics like fast-food, often with the same ingredients. An autobiography would appear in various guises about every two years, but his *Now I See* (1933) deserves a special place amongst conversion stories. He was an editor's despair: quotations unchecked, endless repetitions and misspellings in the untidiest of typescripts ever submitted. The package was shoddy but there was nothing shoddy about Arnold's mind. He was as agile in the upper regions of religious controversy as he was on the ski-slopes of Switzerland which he had made his own. He was a whole-hogger in his Romanism and I was tempted to tease him with such questions as: 'Who does God like best – a good Protestant or a bad Catholic?' He would scorn the 'blue domers', as he called those who drew spiritual inspiration without dogmatic content from the deep blue skies over the mountains, but there can be no doubt that the mysteries of God's creation were also taught wordlessly to him in the Alpine peaks.

Eric Gill came into my life long before he came into the publishing office. He had been one of my gurus in my schooldays. I visited him with Henry John in the summer holidays of 1922, at our own invitation. At that time Eric and his family were living in a community of other artists and craftsmen (a distinction which he would not acknowledge) at Ditchling, nestling under the Sussex Downs. Our first sight of the men of Ditchling was when they lined up on either side of their small chapel to sing the daily office of Compline. Besides Eric there was Hilary Pepler who ran St Dominic's Press. Its productions were hand-set and printed on a hand press on hand-made paper. Others included Laurie Cribb, stone-cutter with Eric; Philip Hagreen, painter; Dunstan Pruden, silversmith; Valentine Kilbride, weaver; George Maxwell, builder; Herbert Shore, metalworker.

David Jones was a diminutive figure amongst these older, mostly bearded, men in their working smocks. They sang Vespers every evening. The Gregorian chant flowed back and forth across the aisle with the murmuration of little waves on a sandy seashore. It was a new wonder for me. I now liken it to my first vision of Chartres Cathedral, coming round the corner of a narrow street to the great *place*. Henry and I had only known the boisterous hymn-singing at Stonyhurst. Eventually we were bedded down in the sweet-smelling hay of the stables. We were awakened at dawn by the pissing and stamping of our only companion, a plough horse.

David took us in hand next morning and introduced us to his companions in their various habitats. Eric and his wife Mary – so benign as to be almost beatified – gave us lunch and sent us on our way. I left enriched to an extent which I never imagined just then.

Some four years later David walked into the Sheed & Ward office and there began the deepest and most lasting friendship of my life.

In 1928 Eric Gill moved to Pigotts, a rambling farmstead on a hill near High Wycombe in Buckinghamshire. Eric was my senior by twenty-four years. That is a big gap when one is seventeen. But he stayed young all his life, and, by the time I was in my middle twenties, we were more like contemporaries. He entered with enthusiasm into my launching of *Order* (of which more later), writing for it and introducing me to likely supporters. I brought him into the Sheed & Ward list and arranged for the firm to be selling agents for books printed at Pigotts.

Ditchling had dissolved in an unhappy difference of view in its community. Pigotts came to be a weekend home-from-home for me. In those years one was alert to everything that life had to offer, negotiating a minefield of ideas and emotions in a no-man's land between opposed trenches: those of my faith and those of the world outside. Pigotts seemed to me a safe billet if ever there was one.

It was built on three sides of a large yard. Eric's house backed onto the big barn, ideal for his sculpture; between the two was a little chapel and his main workroom. Across the yard were the cottages of his two sons-in-law and their families: Denis Tegetmeier, engraver on copper and wood, married to Petra, and René Hague, married to Joan. René, a printer, set his type by hand and printed on a hand press. He worked with a sensibility bordering on genius and his books have a personality all their own.

By the early 1930s Eric was at the height of his powers: renowned for his sculpture, his lettering on stone, his engraving on wood and his type-designs. As if all this was not enough, he was writing polemical essays on aesthetics and social subjects of every kind. I would often sit side by side whilst he bent over a magnifying glass as he engraved on wood. He liked to talk as he worked, and talk mostly meant argument.

The themes repeated themselves – as Eric did so often in his writing: the essential evil of industrialism and, paradoxically, the values of Communism, the workers' ownership of the means of production, and so on.

But as the 1930s wore on our arguments were increasingly divisive. Eric and I were in constant touch. I have no record of the period but a letter of mine to him, reprinted in Robert Speaight's *The Life of Eric Gill* (1966) shows a growing gulf. I wrote:

> What we have to bother about is not so much that the present thing is awry, but how, in detail, it is wrong and to be righted. I don't believe there's a gang of arch-crooks who know it's wrong and want

to keep it so for their gain; man in so far as he is an economist is a bewildered little creature constantly upset by interruptions: as a creature of lust, or pride, or avarice, or imagination working outside the practical order ... I believe that insecurity, wars, injustices of all sorts are his chronic condition – and as the remote cause of all that, I posit the consequences of the Fall! There will never be plenty so long as there is jealousy, and there will ever be jealousy. I don't agree with your clean-sweepiness. A certain social security, an absence of squalor, is the best that can be hoped for; a thing built up slowly from trading, as it always has been, but on world trading as it now must be, hence on international lending – I see no way out of it so long as there are seven million people in a few square miles of England who need shirts and skirts, acres of cotton-fields in India to provide the stuff, if it can be got in, if the crop can be sown, if the sowers can be fed, if the shirt-weavers can feed them in expectation of their shirts, if the shirt-wearer has the cash.

According to Robert Speaight I went on to argue that since the profits of the banks largely went in salaries and dividends – that is to say to consumers – why should they complain and why should anyone scorn the 'consumer society'?

Was I disputing with my guru of ten years back? There remains for me and always will the essential Eric: a man of passion and compassion, of joy and jokes. But all this was becoming clouded over and confused by the polluted thought of the time, and both of us were in a foreboding mist. Eric, the one-time Fabian, had been a Distributist at Ditchling; he was on the verge of Communism in 1936, entirely convinced, if not duped, by its propaganda about the Spanish Civil War. The Dominican tertiary of Pigotts was now drawing ecclesiastical fire on account of the erotic element in his engraving as well as for his left-wing journalistic connections.

There seemed to be creeping into him a spirit of impatience: agonised and arrogant by turns so that his denunciations and accusations turned to tirades far removed from the lucid judgements of years back. Maybe there was also something of a masculine menopause.

Anyway we were both heavily overloaded with work; there

was no leisure for contact and discussion. And we were seeing different signs of the times.

But a man like Eric never dies in memory or consciousness – or in conscience for that matter. We talk in a parrot way of the communion of saints but some should manifest it more than most. They are companions at unexpected moments, counsellors when we have no living equivalents. The Catholic faith has no room for death in the secular sense. As Spanish realism has it, the dead are *presente*.

I wrote the above about Gill before the publication of a new biography by Fiona MacCarthy (1991). By and large it is a good piece of work. But she extended her researches to some private diaries of Gill's which, unwarrantably, had been sold to a unversity library in the United States. They revealed a sexual life, occasionally deviant to say the least, which, I know, totally surprised his closest friends. Such sporadic doings are inexcuseable in civilised society but they are pardonable by God who would have spared the whole of Sodom if there had been only one just man in the city. A man is not merely made up of fleeting passions and obsessions, and a biographer betrays him when these are dredged up from the detritus of his past. It were better to follow the example of Jesus who, finding a bunch of 'righteous' men prepared to stone to death a woman taken in adultery, asked 'Which of you is without sin?' – and any sin, to him, was something hideous beyond words. None dared to throw the first stone and they all shuffled off. He began to write in the sand (possibly a catalogue of their horrible and secret acts), but he wrote in the shifting sand, not for the Sunday papers.

I have left my portrayal of Eric Gill untouched.

5
New Frontiers

In the 1920s I went to live with my oldest brother, Charles, a doctor with a general practice in Chelsea and a specialised one at the Tavistock Clinic for nervous diseases in Bloomsbury. At that time these districts were catchment areas for two very different streams. They occasionally mingled in the fairly frequent parties which seemed to spring up spontaneously at our house in St Leonard's Terrace, Chelsea.

My first contacts with Bloomsbury baffled rather than shocked me. I could make little of its denigrating approach to so many values that I held to be sacred. After Paris, I was not awed by Bloomsbury intelligence. Its religious requirements appeared to be satisfied by Frazer's *Golden Bough* and its sexual mores seemed to derive from the Trobriand Islanders. Douglas McClean, our 'pet atheist', as I would call him, was a gifted doctor, a frequent guest. He was an enjoyable sparring parter in any argument – and, as Manning remarked, 'All arguments are basically theological.' I had not met many avowed atheists at that time and they fascinated me like creatures in the more obscure cages and terraces of the Zoo. I could not make out how or why they existed.

For that matter I had had virtually no contact with Protestants. When first introduced to John Betjeman, my spontaneous greeting was, 'You're the first Protestant I've ever met!' I was breaking out of Catholic exclusivity to my benefit. One of John's great Oxford friends, 'Cracky Clonmore' as he always called him, brought us together. Billy Clonmore was a man without guile; he had resigned his Anglican curacy in the East End of

London to become a Catholic, to the rage of the great Protestant house of Howard, Earls of Wicklow. In vain the old earl had sent a succession of moustachioed low churchmen to warn Billy off his chosen course. Billy went on; John did not, staying in his Protestant world where not a little fantasy prevailed. But he and his poetry were always a delight to me and I bitterly resented Evelyn Waugh's constant hounding of the man with threats of hellfire. They brought real distress to John and his wife Penelope – who later became a Catholic as if to the manner born.

My 'pet atheist' was living with a lovely woman, a writer and illustrator of children's books. The idea of cohabitation was strange to me, not a normality as it has now become. Homosexuality was another oddity to me. It had been sublimated quite effectively at Stonyhurst, and I had missed Oxbridge where the opposite of sublimation was the fashion. So that the appearance of Cedric Morris and his saturnine lover, another painter, at St Leonard's Terrace was another novelty of a type with which I rapidly became familiar. André Gide's *Corydon* – one of my Paris books – had prepared the ground. Personally I was much more attracted to 'a world full of he's and she's' which Eric Gill so constantly extolled.

Those were halcyon days at St Leonard's Terrace. There were occasional late-night parties, as well as a regular recurrence of Saturday lunches. Normally the company would begin with the two friends that we had boarding with us. The longest inhabitants were Francis Howard (now Lord Howard of Penrith) and Alick Dru – who was embarking on his immense task and achievement of learning Danish and translating Kierkegaard. Both were from Downside as also was Jack Hamson, a frequent guest, who ended up as Professor of International Law at Cambridge. (The line with Downside was wonderful for me, leading as it did to friendship with Abbot Chapman, David Knowles and Hubert van Zeller.) Fr D'Arcy was a fairly regular attendant, coming down from Oxford where he was Master of Campion Hall. He would produce undergraduates to diversify the company, like Wysten Auden, Stephen Spender and Robert

Speaight, as well as strays in his collection of neophytes. I remember particularly Georges Cattaui, an attaché at the Egyptian Embassy, almost a reincarnation of Marcel Proust, on whom he came to publish more than one learned commentary. David Jones was a regular luncher, and Harman Grisewood, then an announcer at the BBC, in the days of Reith.

★   ★   ★

In these years, before there were even rumours of war, publishing absorbed my working day. Things were different in the evenings. My brother Charles had married and moved to Birmingham (to found a child-guidance clinic which still bears his name). I was solitary and gregarious at the same time.

There were cocktail parties everywhere, some of them hunting grounds for literary talent. During 'the season' there was one great ball after another. From my modest quarters in Chelsea I would emerge, like a butterfly from a chrysalis, in white tie and tails, for these events. They were often given by hostesses scarcely known to me. I discovered that I was on some sort of hostess register; my entry read: 'Smart young man, dances well, safe in taxis.' I have my doubts about the total accuracy of this description. But I avoided any deep commitments. I did not see the finality of marriage as appropriate for me, nor any *liaison dangereuse*. I lived, nevertheless, in a state of fluctuating affections, finding some safety in numbers. 'No strings, no connections' was one of the theme songs of the time.

When there were no balls there were always night-clubs. The Gargoyle, the Café Anglais and Hell were habitual havens. In each I could claim a bottle of whisky with my name on the label, on which waiters would make pencil marks marking a night's intake, to be charged accordingly. This was a simple evasion of the licensing laws, since the bottle had been bought during permitted hours. 'Hell' was my favourite haunt – a startling address for taxi drivers.

'The Blues' or negro spirituals was the sort of music that I cared to hear. My education hardly extended to classical music, extending not much further than the hypnotic rhythm of Ravel's Bolero and the haunting melody of Dvorak's New World Symphony. But then came many visits to Don Giovanni. The first of them had its own incidence. To get there I boarded a bus and clambered to the top. The only other occupant was a young man up front. I sat near him.

'Does this bus go to Sadlers Wells?'

'To the very door,' he said and we chatted awhile. When we arrived at the opera house we both disembarked. My next sight of him was conducting the orchestra. It was Benjamin Britten, youthful in those days.

It was in such gatherings that occurred the spontaneous generation of an idea for a review dedicated to reforming the Catholic Church, at least in its local manifestation. To me, at any rate, the Church was the *Sacramentum Mundi*, the outward sign of inward grace, intended to permeate human existence. I saw it, however, as frail and flawed in many ways, almost an obstacle to faith.

I called the review *Order*. The first number was published in May 1928. I wanted it to be anonymous, so I published it from a Monomark address: the arguments were to carry their own weight and not to be accepted on account of authorship. It seemed to me that ecclesiastical materialism was at the root of our troubles, whereby churchmen produced codes and conventions as *means* which eventually served to obscure the *end* or purpose of the whole thing. Thus we were up against, dismayed by, the hideous aesthetic expressions of modern religion: the *bondieuserie* which had no relationship with the legacy of the Middle Ages and the Renaissance.

In the first issue Eric Gill struck a blow at what he called Repository Art. Modern methods of religious education were another target: Jack Hamson wrote a piece which was taken very seriously by the Bishops' Conference. Much as I admired the character, with all its bluff and bluster, of Hilaire Belloc, I had doubts about his effectiveness as a credible apologist – I did not agree with his dictum that, 'Europe is the Faith, and the Faith is Europe.' Denis Brogan handled the matter in trenchant fashion. We were taking on all the sacred cows.

Ironically, as it turned out for me, I put most of the blame for the deplorable state of affairs on Catholic journalism, and I singled out *The Tablet* as the most culpable. The proprietor was *ex officio* the Archbishop of Westminster. Cardinal Manning had bought the paper from its lay founder and editor just before the First Vatican Council in 1870, possibly fearing that *The Tablet* would be too liberal and Cisalpine. The new editor was Manning's appointee, as were his successors down to Ernest Oldmeadow, the appointee of Cardinal Bourne. Oldmeadow had been a free churchman and had all the zeal of a convert sharpening his old antagonism to the Anglican Church. As a result *The Tablet* was sectarian and puritanical, pompous and parochial. Nevertheless, it was, in journalistic terms, authoritative and as such widely quoted by the media. This seemed to me grossly detrimental to the Church. I attacked it mercilessly, without, of course, the slightest idea that I would myself be in the editorial chair forty years on.

David Jones identified himself with our group by a wood engraving for the cover: a unicorn symbolically prancing in an enclosed garden to 'cleanse the waters', as in the medieval myth. The first issue had a bombshell effect, sold 2,000 copies in two weeks and was reprinted. Nobody save the actual contributors could identify the editor or anyone else in the enterprise.

The Catholic establishment was taken by surprise and began to take stock of itself. Ronald Knox, addressing the assembled bishops, referred to an article on religion in a review which he preferred not to name: the message had got through.

I had called the paper *Order* for that seemed to me what it should be all about. A sentence from the *Summa contra Gentiles* was at the masthead:

According to established popular usage, which the Philosopher considers should be our guide in the naming of things, those are called wise who put things into their right order and control them well.

The title had nothing to do with the New Order of German or Italian nationalism emerging at that time. In fact, it astonishes me now what little attention my group – with the exception of Christopher Dawson – paid to politics as such. 'A fish rots at the head first,' as Daudet remarked, and it was to the intellect that we addressed ourselves: the main area of concern. Burke, writing of the 'moral imagination', saw it as a power which 'aspires to the apprehending of right order in the soul and right order in the commonwealth'. That was what we were after. It is, after all, the basis of the *philosophia perennis* which Maritain had revealed to me as a living tradition, over and against materialism in its myriad forms.

There was, of course, more than a whiff of Paris in the review. So many books had been buried in my head; they were beginning to sprout. Apart from that, Julien Green wrote on 'The Present Position of Catholics' in the last two issues of the review, a scathing attack on bourgeois Catholicism.

Paris had its own equivalent of *Order* in *Cahiers 1929*, which gave us a free advertisement: '*Abonnez-vous à Ordre ... le* Cahier 1929 *de Londres*'! It was a compliment considering that the *Cahier* had Maritain, Berdyaev, Mauriac, Bernanos and Fumet among its contributors. On its title page there was a message from Henri Massis whose *Défense de l'Occident* had greatly impressed me. What he wrote seemed directly addressed to my group:

> *Ah, mes amis, nous avons du travail plein les mains! Il y a l'unité morale de l'Europe à refaire, les conditions d'un langage commun à retrouver, la philosophie de l'ordre à répandre, la notion de l'homme et de Dieu à rendre manifeste dans les idées et dans les moeurs!*

Our marching orders could not have been put better, but I never met Massis in Paris. Twelve years after those lines were written,

I happened to be walking in the lovely moorish garden of Gregorio Marañon's house outside Toledo. It was one of those Sunday afternoons when his friends from all over the intellectual world would gather: a liberal oasis in Franco's dictatorship. I was with a diminutive Frenchman whose name I had not caught. I was telling him about my Paris days and said, 'I'm only sorry that I never met Massis ...' He stopped me short with some surprise. '*Mais je suis Massis*,' he protested. From his writings I had pictured a lion-headed giant of a man. This, I am sure, was his spirit; I was dumbfounded and delighted to meet him in the flesh.

Something of the flavour of *Order* may be conveyed by extracts from 'An Introductory Restraining Panic,' my first editorial. It now reads to me as rather bumptious, self-assured and pedantic, but I was making a foray into untravelled territory and needed all the confidence that I could summon up.

> ... We are not interested in the sins of individuals. We are not even interested in the mental weaknesses of individuals, except insofar as they are the type and symbol, or the executives, of some larger body of opinion ... We cannot insist too strongly on the necessity of not regarding *Order* as the work of *illuminés*; we fail if our point of view is regarded as abnormal. Contributors to this journal should not be professional scribblers, but people kept busy by routine life, constantly in touch with the trivial, compelled to muster their thoughts and set them down on paper at odd moments, for preference in buses and trains where the only works of reference are the plain faces of their fellow passengers. *Il y a une maison, une lampe, une soupe, du vin, des pipes, derrière toute oeuvre importante de chez nous.*
>
> ... *Order* is at present a latent idea, we want to make it an experiment done publicly, to test its reaction to hot air and a cold reception and wet blankets and hard heads ... if only we may make one man for one moment think more than is his wont ... then will there be something accomplished.

Four issues of *Order* were produced between May 1928 and November 1929 when I decide to close it down. This was not for lack of support but for personal reasons. I thought that I had reached the limit of my perception at various points. I was not afraid to go further. 'Ten thousand difficulties do not make one doubt,' as Newman said, but they do sometimes call for deeper investigation and there was little time for that with the increasing demands of publishing.

I was able, however, to enlist the help of Christopher Dawson as co-editor of a series of *Essays in Order* – little books of 100 pages or so which took *Order* deeper into the heartland of contemporary problems.

I little knew that Christopher was going to be such a formative influence on my mind when we first met in 1928. It was at Hartlington Hall near Skipton in Yorkshire, the family home which he had inherited. Of that Victorian pile I can only remember cavernous cold rooms and a library where Christopher would sit most of the time in a high-backed armchair with books all round it, knee-deep. The only light in the place was his wife Valerie, tall and beautiful with unaffected charm. She ministered to husband, family and their guest with an easy devotion and would slip in and out of the pervading gloom at unexpected moments.

I had gone there to discuss editorial details about *Progress and Religion*, that seminal work which headed one of Sheed & Ward's first lists, in 1929. I soon discovered a disarming characteristic of Christopher's, which was to assume that one was as familiar with the piles of books that enveloped him as he was himself: an assortment ranging from St Jerome to James Joyce.

'Origen is really not quite right about the Fall, is he?' The voice came curiously deep from such a slight figure. Low, monotonous, all its sparkle was in what it said, without emphasis or excitement but new-minted. He would talk about the Fathers of the Church as if they were the familiars of a senior common room and I never knew him to be short of an answer to any question under the sun. For all his learning he had a warm and sensitive heart which showed in the sudden *mirada* of his light brown eyes. It showed also in the almost querulous and constant complaint that he went unrecognised in the world of letters and especially by his own Church. True, honours came later – a chair at Harvard, an appointment to the Gifford lectureship – but he never could quite understand that his knowledge and his vision put him out of touch with ordinary people and that he could not expect a large following.

One had to play midwife to Christopher's books as they neared the end of their gestation. This involved trips to Devon – where he had moved from the cold of the north – giving encouragement and psychological energy which left one quite drained. But it was all worthwhile; tempering my somewhat impetuous nature, opening new horizons for me. We worked together as editors of *Essays in Order* which included such diverse minds as Maritain's, the Russian philosopher Berdyaev, Germans such as Peter Wust, Theodore Haecker and Ida Coudenhove, and from home, Herbert Read and E. I. Watkin. Christopher greatly helped me over a large book of essays on St Augustine by various hands which I edited for the fifteenth centenary of that portentous Doctor of the Church.

By the spring of 1929 I was deeply involved in producing *Order*. (Much of our relationship was conducted by letter during these years and I am indebted to Christopher's daughter, Mrs Christina Scott, for permission to publish extracts from our correspondence.) A long letter written from Catalonia thanks Christopher for his 'excellent' article. I enclosed a published essay of Aldous Huxley's: 'It seems to me he is in the running for discovering the "more abundant life".' I tell Christopher to quote his case, to 'encourage him along the life-worshipping line'.

I must have had Huxley very much in my sights at that time as the following year (2 February 1930) I write from the Savile Club' '... in half an hour I have to go and dine with Aldous Huxley under the hawk eye of Ottoline Morrell, intent on fomenting religious discussion. Ye Gods!' In another letter I expound my ideas on the military virtues, referring to Peguy and

Psichari and 'battalions of the French with their mystic militarism'. I also enlarge on the need for a businessman to 'be an artist in his business; this is his natural job. Then he must have a supernatural motive; that is his Christian job. The supernatural motive makes for "*le sacrement du moment present*" (or some such phrase of Caussade's).' The lessons of Paris were evidently still in my mind, but I was lecturing a man seventeen years older than myself and infinitely more wise.

Later that year (September 1930) there was less pontificating and more discipleship. I had come back from staying with friends in a house by Lake Como:

> ... a huge holiday, knowing only the sun and the water and the time of the next meal and the hours of gentle talk about nothing in particular ... There's a strange flutter and pounding in me which I dread because it means to say Create ... I pull up and tell myself that I am perilously near to writing a novel ... But after all I think it better to be silent and not add to the confusion of tongues, to remember one's creatureliness and the creatures near in my affections, to 'make the patient easy' when possible and pray for him when not. Chain up the imagination, but loose the intellect, working in a certain order of practical affairs and attend to the teaching of men of tradition, knowledge and principles quite clear, who will write economically and to the point. Surely this is right? I mean let me be a publisher – a porter of other people's goods ...

David Jones engraved another unicorn rampant for the *Essays*. The animal had become a symbol for my publishing effort. David, typically, had come across the writing of one John of Hesse, priest, who had written his account of a pilgrimage to Jerusalem at the end of the fifteenth century. He noted:

> Near the fields of Helyon there is a river called Marah, the water of which is very bitter, into which Moses struck his staff and made the water sweet, so that the Children of Israel might drink. And even in our times, it is said, venomous animals poison this water after the setting of the sun, so that the good animals cannot drink of it. But in the morning, comes the Unicorn and dips his horn into the stream,

Eric Gill
(c. 1924)

David Jones
(c. 1964)

Christopher Dawson (c. 1952)

driving the poison from it so that the good animals can drink there during the day.

To me this was an allegory of everything that I believed in. There seemed to me a stream of clear thought seeping through the world from ancient Greece, and long before, which had come to be poisoned by sophistries and prejudices and passions throughout history. To me the unicorn symbolised the Holy Spirit coming to visit and clarify these turbulent waters.

One was immensely conscious of a welter of ideas, that these in their turn generated attitudes which generated conflicts at every level, from the personal to an international enmity. One's own self was a microcosm of all this. Just as one's own self, in one's own authentic experience, was conscious of the Spirit within one calling '*Abba*, father,' so it seemed should society be, for mankind was me. This identification was neither presumptuous nor despairing, but radically hopeful. I had been relieved to learn that the essential unity of the human race was *de fide*. It followed that every idea can be shared with another, that personal experience has a universal quality, history is always relevant and literature can be an immediate experience. We are not isolated atoms: communication is all.

But what has all this to do with publishing? Well, everything. To me it was always more mission than merchandising. It was proselytism, not propaganda. It was porterage from mind to mind. An endless and exciting prospect had opened up. I was in my element and my incurably optimistic nature persuaded me that everyone else should share it.

Every day in those first years of publishing meant some new discovery: some truth waiting to be disclosed and expressed. It soon became clear that there was a rich mine in Europe to be exploited as well as unsuspected riches among Catholic thinkers in England who only needed some encouragement and an outlet.

If Frank Sheed and I had anything in common it was the conviction that the quality and relevance of a book were what counted in the decision to publish or not to publish. Its financial prospects came second. I was always dismayed to find colleagues in the trade who thought otherwise. There was, however, one chilling and pervasive cloud over this outlook: something of the nature of atomic fall-out blown about by winds in the stratosphere (although in those days, of course, there was no such term in our vocabulary). In endless talk and rumination with friends like David Jones and Christopher Dawson and Harman Grisewood, we would come to face what we called 'the Break' – an alienating event in what was known of our civilisation: more a slow-burner than an event, in fact.

It seemed to us that the Reformation, the age of Revolution and Industrialism had eroded the territory of the sacral in daily living: modern man was losing a vital dimension in his life, the utilitarian motive was self-sufficient; a culture without religion was no culture – and scarcely civilised. The confirmation of this view and the reaction against it came strongly from France and Germany. My Paris novitiate came to bear fruit. Maritain and his friends had made contact with German theologians and philosophers like Romano Guardini, Peter Wust, Theodore Haecker and Karl Adam. Knowing no German, that stream of thought came through to me through the French. It was all the more encouraging with that endorsement.

To catalogue or comment on all this output would be tedious. By 1931, when Sheed & Ward was five years old, we had published 191 different titles at an increasing momentum. David Jones had also provided us with a colophon for the catalogues which was as appropriate as the unicorn for *Essays in Order*: a lovely wood-engraving of 'a stag set free'. Of this, St Bernard of Clairvaux (writing in the twelfth century), who might have had foreknowledge of what we were up to – for such is the communion of saints – wrote:

Its leaps and bounds well typify the ecstasies of the speculative mind; it is able to thread the way through the closest thickets of forests, as such a mind penetrates obscurities of meaning.

In 1932 *The Manchester Guardian*, as it was then called, was the staunch upholder of secularist ideals, virtually Bloomsbury's parish magazine. An accolade from that quarter was as unexpected as it was encouraging:

The firm of Sheed & Ward is devoted to 'penetrating obscurities' mainly in fields of philosophy, theology, history, criticism and sociology. This work is done almost exclusively by Roman Catholic writers but with benefits far beyond the boundaries of that communion. The firm has, in fact, been largely instrumental in bringing the fruits of the intellectual renaissance among Catholics in Europe to the English public. Even in a decade which has seen the rapid rise of many new firms, the progress of Sheed & Ward has had something of the phenomenal ... *Essays of Order* [is] a series whose general aim is to weigh up the possibilities for co-operation and of conflict between the modern world and Catholicism at every point where contact can be established – in the arts, the sciences, philosophy, politics, economics, ethics. Christopher Dawson edits the series, with T. F. Burns, the manager of the firm, and his work, here and elsewhere, has done much to bring Catholicism within the orbit of the modern Englishman.

We had at least established a beachhead.

Of course there was a human and sometimes hilarious background to all this effort. We were only two men thick when we started, apart from a bookkeeper-manager, a traveller, a typist and two packers. In the office, editorial reinforcement was clearly required. So I began to recruit what came to be known as my 'Foreign Legion'. They were mostly just down from Oxbridge and waiting to embark on their various careers.

There was Douglas Carter, a Wykehamist classical scholar and a convert of Fr D'Arcy's. He had a detached, incisive wit and was marked for the priesthood where he came to have the reputation of being somewhat rigid in his views; he was never happy about Vatican II and never reconciled to my policy in *The*

Tablet, but we stayed friends to his dying day. Another D'Arcy convert was Jimmy Oliver who had read modern languages and mastered French literature. He went on to write novels which deserved more success than they achieved. His studies of Balzac, Gibbon and Patmore are still worth reading.

There was Alick Dru, invaluable with his awe-inspiring knowledge of German literature and gearing himself for his great translation of Kierkegaard. Billy Clonmore also joined 'the Legion' and was immensely helpful for a couple of years before he went off to found his own firm in Dublin. These and others came and went in a mixed atmosphere of hard work and hilarity.

To have some idea of the receiving end of publishing, the booksellers, I took time off to work as a traveller. My reception by booksellers when I displayed my unfamiliar wares was discouraging. Once, I recall, I went to Manchester in a dreary cold week of Lent. The taxi at the station sized me up: 'Commercial?' he asked. I agreed to the description and indicated that he could take me wherever 'commercials' were accustomed to go. In a dreary back-street he pulled up opposite what appeared to be a commercial hotel. A ring at the door produced a buxom lady scantily clad in a kimono. She was more perceptive than the taximan: 'You don't want this place, darling. It's a tart house.' The taximan took me on. 'You should have explained,' he said.

The next place was pretty rum. A kindly woman simply said, 'First floor, first on the right' and there I was dumped in a bleak bedroom with no more ado. Things livened up, however. I heard the strains of a harmonium playing some music across the corridor. I went across and peeped through the half-open door. There was a man in a priestly soutane playing before an altar where twelve crossed palms were arranged in brass jars. 'Do come in and look,' said the harmonium player. He gripped my arm and pointed to one palm which was bent over its jar.

'The twelfth always falls down: *Judas*,' he said.

'Are you are Catholic priest?' I asked.

'Well yes, I am an Old Catholic priest.'

I remembered Dr Dollinger and his schismatic separation at the First Vatican Council when Old Catholics dissented from papal infallibility. We had a very amicable and earnest conversation far into the night. It was only interrupted by the entrance of a bright girl asking, 'Can I go to Holy Name for Benediction, daddy?'

'Of course, my dear!' The Holy Name was a neighbouring Catholic church.

Next morning, after a lavish bacon-and-eggs breakfast served by the woman of the previous evening who presented the bill and departed, I was left alone and explored the ground floor. There I discovered a dank darkened room with a notice turned to the wall announcing: 'Spiritualist seances every Wednesday at 8pm.' It was an appropriate penetration into foreign territory which I relished with apostolic zeal.

Happy as I was in my work, my position at Sheed & Ward became more anomalous. I had the power without the responsibility, which, as Mr Baldwin observed, is the prerogative of a harlot. I was in my element when both Sheed as well as Ward (Maisie, his wife) were away – which was a lot of the time, either in the United States or Australia (and there was no air travel for such distances). But I realised, from finding the firm apparently broke in New York, that I had no idea of its resources and thus its viability. I asked to be taken into partnership but Sheed told me that he wished to keep the firm 'a family concern'. We parted in friendly fashion – at least to all appearances – in January, 1936.

6

At the Sign of the Ship

To make a change turned out to be no problem. Just across Paternoster Row was the great centenarian house of Longman, Green & Co. It had a long (but now lost) tradition of Catholic as well as Anglican publishing, including the standard edition of Newman. I happened to know Bobbie Longman, the likeable head of the firm, and decided to offer him my services. I walked across the road and came back with the job that I wanted.

The change in ethos was complete. I stepped into an almost Victorian establishment which might have been dealing with any commodity but happened to be producing books, mostly textbooks. The general list for such a large firm was sparse and without character; the Catholic list had virtually withered away. Within six months or so my leading authors at Sheed & Ward were beginning to come across to Longmans. For the Longmans general list I brought in friends for at least one-off appearances. Among them was Evelyn Waugh with *Waugh in Abyssinia* (1936) (the punning title was my fault and we both regretted it) and Graham Greene with *Lawless Roads* (1939).

I had fun helping Eleanor Smith with her memoirs, *Life's a Circus* (1938). She was an eternal high-spirited tomboy delighting in the company of gypsies and circus folk. We saw a lot of each other, without the intrusive pangs of sex, to our mutual relief. The war came and I saw nothing and heard nothing of her for a year. On my first leave from Spain we went off one night to dine at the Mirabelle. Suddenly there was a hush and a stir in that exotic restaurant. Churchill entered with Brendan Bracken and some other cronies. He came straight across to our table, smiling broadly. Eleanor's father, Lord Birkenhead, had been one of his closest friends. It was in the very darkest days of the war and Britain was facing the enemy 'alone', to use a word from a famous broadcast of his. 'Well, my dear, I'm glad to see that at least we have the gypsies with us.' Eleanor died before my next leave but that memory has stuck with me, typical of her starlit life.

Longmans became all-absorbing. Their book-design was drab beyond belief. I befriended the production manager and he gratefully let me take it over, content to cope with all the calculations and general spadework.

I set my sights beyond the Catholic list. The old Longmans literary tradition had virtually disappeared. The directors were primarily business men and (except for Bobbie Longman) more concerned with the vast opportunities of the educational market, expanding worldwide, than with their fine, largely lost, record in general literature and fiction (shades of Trollope!). The literary adviser, Eric Gillet, was a genial relaxed crony of Jack Squire with his *London Mercury* and their cricket friends. Eric was grateful for my enthusiasm and for the books of established authors which I had so quickly brought to the firm. With Bobbie's agreement, the old colophon of a sailing ship went back on title pages and there were new horizons. If I could not contract Graham Greene and Evelyn Waugh for novels, there were possibilities of non-fiction from them in the future. I knew that I had strong financial backing and that we could compete with the best. But the war demolished all these dreams. After the war Longmans virtually lost its identity in a giant merger, concentrating on the educational market; no place for me, I decided.

Although my friendship with Graham and Evelyn extended long before and long after my Longmans days, this seems to be the place to recall it, at a point where I felt their stimulus most keenly. The impact of both men was a cumulative one, over decades, and it seems better to treat it as a whole than dispersed through different times and isolated occasions.

I am not sure which came first into my experience: *The Man Within* (1929) or the man himself. Graham Greene's first published novel, its title and quotation from Sir Thomas Browne, 'There is another man within me who is angry with me,' at once struck a chord: one of self-recognition or the recognition of a kindred spirit, which is much the same thing. That was in June 1929: Graham was twenty-four, I was twenty-three.

At any rate, he leapt into my landscape like a leprechaun, as it seemed to me: witty, evasive, nervous, sardonic, by turns. He stood out in the company we both kept in those days, which was mainly of publishers and authors, joyfully joined in plans and projects. Nothing was stereotyped, nothing predictable, for the world as we knew it was free – little knowing of its bondage to come.

Graham, like many young authors, was also a publisher's reader at the time. He worked for Eyre & Spottiswoode, whose board members tended to conclude their meetings at the Lamb and Flag, a pub near the Garrick. Graham seemed to me to have a spotlight on him, although his companions were by no means shadowy figures and I recall them all with affection. There was Douglas Jerrold, the chairman of the company and a tall, saturnine figure. He was all of a right-wing piece, the editor of a strongly conservative monthly, a vocal critic of the Bloomsbury set, a Counter-Reformation Catholic, a high hard-headed Tory, a one-time Treasury official with a computer for a mind in that small head of his. Through some Secret Service connection, incidentally, he later was to play an important part in flying General Franco from the Canaries to the African mainland in a British chartered aircraft, to start the military revolt which led to the Spanish Civil War. (Juan Belmonte, the king of bullfighters, once remarked to me: 'Unless it is proved to the contrary, I assume all Englishmen are in the Intelligence Service.')

In contrast to Jerrold was his close colleague Sir Charles

Petrie; an owlish, rotund and bearded baronet, a learned historian but as much at home in the Lamb and Flag as in the Carlton Club. Frank Morley made up the trio: a huge Harvard and Rhodes scholar who adopted England as his own and had settled near its heart, in Buckinghamshire. He was a giant of a man with all the gentleness and tolerance of a big mind and body.

In such company Graham stood out, an incurable eccentric for whom there were no comfortable assumptions. The man within was not only angry but impatient and insatiably curious. Anyway, we two seemed to hit it off. He invited me to his house on Clapham Common. Personally I was sceptical at that time about the possibility of any permanent matrimonial happiness and Graham's home came as a complete surprise. His gentle and beautiful wife had it all arranged with such care. There was a serenity of order in every detail: so different from everything that I had been able to observe of Graham himself. The old song of the Silver Sty came to mind: 'There was a lady loved a swine; Honey said she; Honk said he.' Not that there was anything gross about Graham – he was all sensibility and courtesy – but this couple existed in two totally different circumstances in the sense that the Spanish philosopher Ortega y Gasset would say: 'I am I – and my circumstance.' It is an almost irremediable condition. Paradoxically it may be cured by love which both blinds one and opens one's eyes. But Graham at the time was desperately writing, not for himself, or from any urge for self-expression, but to keep his home together. It is not surprising to read now, in his published life, of his passionate love and unconditional devotion for the girl he spotted in Blackwell's bookshop – as Dante spotted Beatrice at the bridge. But he was himself *and* his circumstance, with its demanding conditions.

We were both too busy to see much of each other but there would come the occasional telephone call: 'Let's go to Limehouse tonight, there's a ballet of Chinese nudes at the local theatre.' This sort of exultant *nostalgie de la boue* never appealed to me.

A great chance came for both of us in 1938 when Graham had

an instinct to write about the Mexican revolution of President Callas. He wanted to study the president's pitiless persecution of the Church at first hand. His own publisher and others were not interested: for them Mexico was far away and religion a hazy notion. Graham and I saw it quite differently and I was able to persuade my somewhat bovine board at Longmans to accept my view and come up with £500 – quite a sum in those days for a writer untried in this field. The result was all that I had hoped for – *The Lawless Roads* – Graham's account of his tour, a very graphic and devastating exposure of what he had seen. Better still, it gave him all the material he needed for his first breakthrough and still his best novel, *The Power and the Glory* (1939).

Unfortunately for me Graham's regular publisher had an option on all his fiction so I could not take on the novel – but I have ever since been glad to have helped to make it possible. The 'whisky priest' has become part of human experience. Many years later quite a different sort of priest with his distinct character and his own wide human appeal emerged from Graham's imagination. This was Monsignor Quixote in a book of that name. It began as a fragment and only acquired a framework in the course of writing. I was editing *The Tablet* and Graham offered a piece for the Christmas issue of 1972. He thought at the time that it would not develop into anything. But the following year came another piece: a story with a shape evolving on its own, a person emerging. But after that Graham wrote to say that he had come to a halt and would have to leave the story unfinished. I wrote to tell him that the next Christmas issue would be my last and just hoped that there would be one more instalment to mark my own *finale*. Graham's response was typically generous, he set to work again and virtually rounded off the story. So *Monsignor Quixote* was created against all odds. It was always a stimulus to me that I had Graham's moral support and general approval throughout my editing of *The Tablet*. It was shown in innumerable ways and not least by his agreeing to become a trustee of *The Tablet* Trust. To go back a bit: just after the publication of *The Power and the Glory* the Second World War began. We did not see or hear from each other for more than five years after a brief spell together in the Ministry of Information. The break was mended with a lunch in Rules in Covent Garden. It was now my turn to introduce a wife. Our shared love of Spain and its people was apparently infectious. It infected Graham and eventually bore fruit as acknowledged by him in his dedication of *Monsignor Quixote*. From the 1950s onward Graham and I inhabited different worlds: an occasional exchange of signals kept us in contact and some sort of contact was important to both of us. It was something like the relationship of old schoolfriends – distanced and familiar. In our case the Church served as our *Alma Mater* and some of the masters we shared were Newman, von Hügel and Unamuno. Loyalty to such figures is not faith but a sort of star-war defence system against the principalities and powers in high places where, as St Paul taught us, is the real warfare.

Some serenity had come to both of us in our eighties and such meetings as a weekend in Antibes towards the end of his life, when there was feasting and a Mass shared in the local church, when we stood at the back like two publicans from the Gospel. We had known each other for sixty years. When Graham came to my eightieth birthday party at home I left him to be devoured by my family and friends. It is not for me to make any judgement of anyone, but in Graham's case I shall always value his life-long resistance to all the temptations of world fame. 'Blessed are the poor in spirit, for they shall see God.'

It must have been in the autumn of 1930 when I first met Evelyn Waugh. The occasion was a dinner *à trois*, with Douglas Woodruff, the host, in his dingy book-laden chambers in Lincoln's Inn. Douglas, with his conspiratorial attitude to life in general and Catholic life in particular, had presumably picked on me as a suitable mentor for this neophyte in the unfamiliar

Catholic milieu that he had recently entered. Mine was not a very different social swim from Evelyn's but, in those days, English Catholics had their own life at different levels; the rest had theirs. That is how it was.

For Evelyn it was the beginning of an exploration that was to end seven years later with marriage in the glades of the Catholic aristocracy. For me it was the beginning of a friendship which gave me joy for many years but which died from lack of repair after the war as our destinies divided. Leaving Lincoln's Inn at midnight we agreed that it was too early to retire. Evelyn proposed a visit to 'The 43' (a night-club of dubious repute which he immortalised as Sink Street in *Vile Bodies*). Here, like Bishop Blougram and Mr Gigadibs, we 'saw truth dawn over the glass's edge', with theological talk unfamiliar to the professional ladies of the establishment, who largely left us to our own devices.

There is a certain scepticism, tolerance and familiarity with sacred things which the Church inculcates in those who have been nourished by her teaching from the cradle. Latecomers often have a different response. Evelyn saw himself as a man who had joined a regiment with traditions and rules which he never questioned. I remember once spending an Easter weekend with him at an inn at Chagford in Devon where he would often go to write undisturbed. He was observing the Lenten fast with rigorous exactitude, bringing to the table and measuring out in ounces what quantity of food was permitted. There were no scales for the drink when I pronounced, to his relief, the Benedictine adage: *Vinum non frangit jejunium* (wine does not break the fast). This kind of literalism was not a joke for Evelyn, and it extended into regions of semi-Manichean moral theology which were at that time in possession of the Roman seminaries, filtering through to the teachers and preachers of the day. Evelyn was in the grip of this situation.

I recall once an argument about sexual *mores*. 'D'Arcy says you can do anything down to the waistline,' announced Evelyn to my stupefaction. How could the fastidious philosopher of *eros* and *agape* have said anything so outrageous? I let it go. Different voices were beginning to be heard, like the Jesuit, Fr C. C. Martindale, and the Dominicans, Gerald Vann and Thomas Gilby. A great spiritual director like Fr Steuart, the Superior of Farm Street, would counsel against excessive austerity. Dom John Chapman, the Abbot of Downside, told me: 'I chastise the spirit, lest it revolt against the flesh' – a joke at the expense of St Paul, no less, but still a piercing intuition.

It was just this ample Catholic vision that I tried to open up for Evelyn. I remember what came to be called the Laxton Synod from the name of the Dominican school where it was held in 1934. A bunch of bright young Dominicans was in charge of a heterogeneous collection of Catholic intellectuals for a weekend retreat. Evelyn attended in a loud check suit, armed with a box of cigars and an ample supply of whisky. The notable neophyte listened to the talks like an earnest schoolboy, to the edification of his improbable companions in Christ.

In a man who came to expose himself as coarse, snobbish, alcoholic, cruel and whore-mongering, there were many features, to me at least, totally redeeming Evelyn. I could recall many acts done privately of compassion and courtesy. One such touched me personally. I was down with a bad attack of flu in my Chelsea studio. Out of the blue came a courier from Fortnum & Mason bearing a case of champagne with the curt instruction from Evelyn to take a bottle a day until cured.

As one of the few who came through unscathed in his often malicious *Diaries* (1976), I can only suppose that we had many moments of hilarity and harmony and a mutual recognition that our religion was more than a defiance of fashion, something other than aestheticism. Religion was a matter of putting roots into reality. Nothing else. This was our tacit bond. So, many years later, I knew that I was not taking a risk when I suggested that Evelyn might edit and reduce the autobiography of an American Trappist monk, Thomas Merton, called *The Seven Storey Mountain*. Merton was nothing if not fundamental in his mystical discovery. I had read nothing like this book except the

Confessions of St Augustine. Here was an Anglo-American who had a vision and a message like no one else in Catholic spiritual writing at the time. Great was my reassurance when Evelyn instantly saw the value of the book, cut it down and edited it with great sensitivity (he calls it an 'enthralling task' in his *Diaries*). We produced a best-seller under the Hopkins title of *Elected Silence* (1948).

We had survived the Second World War in very different theatres though at one point it looked as if we might have been together. Evelyn turned up at the Ministry of Information early in the war. He had fixed an interview for me with some Special Services unit and advised me to, 'Get a haircut ...' I eventually reached the War Office via Trumper's suitably trimmed. Here a bull-necked officer rushed at me with unexpected questions: 'Can you gouge a man's eyes out with your thumbs – *from behind*?' 'Can you find his kidneys with a sharp knife?' I must have failed in these and other questions because I never heard from him again. Anyway, I was soon off on other business in Spain.

Evelyn, seeing the war as a crusade against the Nazi-Communist alliance, was in the highest spirits. The crusade vision soon evaporated when the Soviet Union switched to an alliance with Britain. It resurfaced temporarily in his personal campaign – through hostile reports sent from Yugoslavia to Army headquarters in Cairo – against Tito, but this was quashed by higher authority. In the earlier years of the war, Evelyn's inefficiency as an officer, added to his insufferable behaviour in one officers' mess after another, had led to his constantly being transferred by commanding officers anxious to get rid of him. On his return from the Middle East to London he had become cynical and embittered; I heard about all this from mutual friends and when Evelyn and I met again it was impossible to start where we had left off.

I came back to England in 1946 with a wife and a baby on the way and we made our first home at 1 Victoria Square in the borough of Westminster. Evelyn's fame had been confirmed with *Brideshead Revisited* (1945). He was alternately absorbed in writing and high living, with hard drinking, to the neglect of his wife and family which I found estranging. He had acquired a *persona* with a constant scowling glare alternating with an expression of ineffable boredom. These masks cracked occasionally with a smile which seemed to me a grotesque grimace. But we kept in touch through an occasional lunch and letters mainly about work. I can only recall one visit to his home, Piers Court, when I endured his painful performance as a punctilious country gentleman.

About this time Evelyn asked us to lend our home for a party in honour of Clare Booth-Luce, the glamorous wife of the proprietor of *Time* and *Life*, an ardent convert, when she would meet the Catholic intelligentsia of London. There was a fine mixture of writers and hacks with a sprinkling of selected clergy; the house was awash with champagne; Dr Hyde, so to call the better side of Evelyn, was at his kindliest and most amusing.

The enjoyment of it was spoilt for Mabél and me on the following evening. Robert Speaight, an actor and author of repute, but also, for no known reason, Evelyn's *bête noire*, presented himself at the door with his invitation. It had been dated for the day after the party. We were alone in the house and Bobbie was an old friend; it was painful to see bewildered dismay and misery on his face. If Mr Hyde had contrived a wonderful spree, Dr Jekyll had contrived the last laugh.

We moved in 1952 to Ashley Gardens, a large Victorian flat opposite Westminster Cathedral, to make room for a growing family, and sent out change-of-address notices. Came a postcard from Evelyn: 'I am sorry to see that you have come down in the world.' (It so happened that we lived in a flat just above Mr Harold Wilson and a High Court judge.)

I saw little of him during his last years when he was beset by family and money troubles, and countless other miseries; not the least of them were his religious difficulties over the vernacular Mass and developments in the Church generally. For him it was a purgatorial phase of great interior suffering. But he managed to write, as always, magnificently.

After a luncheon meeting with Evelyn many years back Hilaire Belloc had pronounced: 'The man is Possessed.' That he had a sort of devil within him would explain his moments of mental cruelty and degrading debauchery as well as his hallucinations of Mr Pinfold, but he also had moral courage to a high degree and he never surrendered his ideals. His last Mass was on his last morning.

7

My New-found Land

Probably the best way of getting to know a foreign country is to have work to do there. Tourists concentrate on a country's past – or its pastimes. I went many times to the United States before and after the Second World War in one or other of the Cunard 'Queens', those highly-civilised floating cities complete in themselves where everything – books, food, people and time itself – seemed to take on a new dimension, as if under some spell.

The purpose of these trips was, of course, to buy and sell book rights and talk over future plans on behalf of Sheed & Ward and, later, Burns & Oates. I soon discovered that few of my American friends liked doing business outside a leisurely lunch.

In the early 1930s the American market was the mainstay of Sheed & Ward business, vital to us as a small new publisher. At that time, there was a very large and quite literate Catholic population, but it was short of American authors. Quite different is the situation today when Catholic authorship has made great strides in all fields.

The Newman Press in Westminster, Maryland, looked like becoming my most constant customer and I decided to pay it an overnight visit. I was warmly greeted by the owner, a very tall, stout and courteous character. He had a pear-shaped head, close-cropped, narrowing at the top, and piggy eyes. He was a bachelor and lived in a roomy house served by an old negro couple whom he treated with enormous deference. His warehouse and office were nearby and there was nothing to suggest that he lived outside this orbit. His business was all mail order, largely with the clergy and religious institutions. I doubt if he ever read a book. But he knew what his public wanted. Mr Eckenrode (for such was his Dutch-sounding name) gave Sheed & Ward large orders for books that no New York publisher would look at. We never got on to Christian-name terms – where every other American publisher started – but his total dedication to his trade and his punctilious manners were endearing.

In those days there was still a clutch of old-fashioned Catholic publishers – downtown in Barclay Street, New York – but the second or third generation of owners seemed to be laid back from the daily tasks. They had inherited prosperity and without a pang went into oblivion in the general transformation of the Church. The larger general publishers were beginning to take an interest in modern Catholic writing and I made many friends among them. Foremost of these friends were Sheila (Cudahy) Pelligrini and Bob Giroux. Sheila (from a wealthy family in Chicago) was hard-headed, imaginative, somewhat sardonic, and immensely well read in modern Catholic letters and philosophy. I never met any other American Catholic woman quite like her (if, indeed, any two women are alike) and always enjoyed her company. She is a grandmother now and has retired to Santa Fè, appropriately named. Bob Giroux was another Catholic, a life-long friend of Thomas Merton, a quiet scholarly man and an inveterate operagoer.

Sheila and Bob were both in the front rank of New York publishers. We were building bridges; for them it was a novel experience to meet a Catholic at their own intellectual level. For my part, I came to realise the vast variety of the American way of life: so great and so tolerant that almost any opinion or enterprise could find support somewhere. My ideas may have seemed exotic or eccentric to these new friends, but they were not thereby ruled out of discussion. Religion was not a taboo subject for talk, as in England. Perhaps I had come to Carthage ...

After several of these trips, Sheed decided that, rather than sell our titles to different publishers, we should do the job ourselves through a New York branch of our own. It was presented to me as a *fait accompli*. Sheed simply announced that he had laid the foundations and asked me to start building. I found that we had ground-floor premises on downtown Fifth Avenue, unfurnished except for a couple of bright young girl graduates, innocent of all business ways. Essential office furniture had to be found, stock in trade was on its way from London and eventually a manager. Meanwhile Sheed's friends and acquaintances drifted in, making encouraging noises. A hard-nosed priest from Brooklyn wearing a bowler hat with his Roman collar seemed to be Sheed's principal mentor and was a frequent visitor. We were certainly an oddity in the publishing world so that a launching party and press conference attracted the curious.

After some weeks the manager arrived. He was Hubert Howard, the son of the recently retired British Ambassador lately in Washington and an old friend of mine. Hubert was just down from Cambridge. He had energy, charm and intelligence but was without any experience. I could only show him the ropes – few as they were – and wish him luck, as there was plenty of work waiting for me back in London.

Six months later I went over to New York again to see how Hubert was getting on. He met me on the quay. 'There's no work for you, Tom,' he said cheerfully, 'there's no money for the staff or the rent. I shall have to close down.' I sent two cables: one to my bank, transferring all I had (scarcely over four figures) to the New York account of Sheed & Ward, and another to Sheed to say that unless it was replaced within a week I would wind up the business. The money came from London – without explanation or apology – and we carried on. But it was the beginning of my break with Sheed. I could not manage a business on either side of the Atlantic without any clue as to its resources.

On this trip there were some other bizarre incidents. I had a friend who ran Putnams and I called in one morning before going to lunch with him. His greeting surprised me: 'The Duke of Windsor is in the office, correcting his proofs. I told him you were coming and he very much wants to meet you.' I could not imagine any reason for this but found the duke at work, in shirtsleeves, spreadeagled over a table covered with galley proofs. 'I wanted to see you to take the opportunity of thanking *The Tablet* for what it said about my abdication.' I was taken aback but just remembered how Douglas Woodruff, the editor at the time, had roughly followed the Churchill line, advocating an option to abdication. '*The Tablet* was better than all the rest.' I marvelled at the duke's memory for detail and his interest in an isolated press comment. I explained that I was only a non-executive director at the time but would certainly pass on his message to the editor.

Years later, during the war, in the Casino at Estoril, a haunt of spies and many shady characters at that time (1943), I was playing at one of the roulette tables when a voice behind said, '*Dix mille sur le noir.*' It was the duke's unmistakeable voice. He was on his way, through a minefield of enemy intrigue in Spain and Portugal, to take up his appointment in the Bahamas. He drew me off to a sofa as if I was an old friend and told me of his last audience with the Pope. 'We talked about Communism all the time. He's against it.' The thundering banality of this comment has obscured my memory from anything else he said, but he seemed to be glad to be holding a different conversation from what might be expected from his glitzy friends across the room.

As I have already mentioned, I had managed to secure the British rights of Thomas Merton's work, beginning with *The Seven Storey Mountain* which Evelyn Waugh edited. Fr Louis Merton, as his name was in religion, was a Trappist monk, belonging to a religious order noted for the extreme austerity of its rule. From a minor public school he had gone to Cambridge, and his reputation for loose living followed him to Columbia University. Then came his conversion to the faith and a clear vocation to the

Trappists: the beginning of an extraordinary career. It was a book – coming from the great order of silence – written under orders. It took the United States by storm. But nobody knew Merton nor was allowed to know him except for a few pre-monastic friends. One of these was Naomi Burton who worked for the literary agent Curtis Brown. We became friends in New York and thanks to that I secured the British rights of all Merton's work.

I came to be in constant correspondence with Merton and so exceptionally was admitted to the small company of his visitors. I hardly knew what to expect before I met him: perhaps a stern ascetic who would scour my poor soul like an old saucepan, who would talk of things beyond my comprehension, who would be hawk-high to me, a sparrow. A monk met me at the station in Louisville, Kentucky, and drove me some miles through undulating farmland dotted with tall trees. Eventually we came to a huge and hideous 'modern Gothic' building. Merton met me at the door, a big sunburnt man with the face of a boxer and laughing blue eyes. He explained that there would be vespers and supper and then silence. He would take me to his hermitage next morning. This turned out to be a bungalow specially built for him about half a mile from the monastery where he could work free from the distraction of community life and away from the curious admirers who were always turning up. It was little more than a wooden hut among the trees lined with books and as neat as a ship's cabin.

I was struck first by his light-heartedness, as if life were a bit of a joke. He belittled such of my moral and spiritual difficulties as I felt bound to convey to a holy hermit. 'And don't you *worry* about those things, you're all right. Now tell me about X and Y,' and his talk was of modern poets. He needed no telling, he seemed to have read everything worth reading. He had a positive zest for current ideas but he wasn't overly earnest about anything, as any academic might be: his lodestone was elsewhere. I knew that I was with a man who lived consciously in the presence of God. It is a state as old as Christianity itself.

Spiritual writers through the centuries have maintained that it is within the range of ordinary believers. Tragically it has been lost to sight by the vast majority of modern Catholics. But finding someone living in that Presence is a rare experience. Simply as a by-product it makes for deep and instinctive friendships. The Spaniards long ago spotted this and have a refrain, '*Entre Santa y Santo pared de cal y canto,*' which means that a thick wall is needed to separate a male saint from a female.

Trappist monks take a vow of silence but after the nationwide success of his autobiography Tom Merton never ceased to write. Sometimes he wrote under orders from his superiors in religion with poor results, but his spontaneous output in prose and poetry was magnificent. One could put, for example, his *Seeds of Contemplation* (1949) on a par with Pascal's *Pensées*. For a hermit he was totally *au courant* with modern sociological situations in every continent, witness his *Thoughts of a Guilty Bystander* (1966) and similar works. Towards the end of his life he became increasingly interested in Eastern religions and Buddhism in particular. He died tragically long before his time, on his way to a congress at Bangkok, killed by an electric short-circuit whilst taking a shower. He was the peer of all American Catholic writers of our century.

Another visit to the heartland of America was to Springfield, Illinois. A bright young publisher from New York had left all that glamour and settled in Lincoln's birthplace, acquiring his actual house and furnishing it with Lincolniana collected from all over the country. He had a large family home nearby and a small Catholic publishing office called Templegate. On a surprise visit to London, long before my visit, he had taken over a large stock of Burns & Oates titles that had found no publisher in the United States. For me they were 'bread and butter' books: solid, slow-selling spiritual stand-bys. He had the imagination to see this and take them *en bloc*. The visit to his house was a delight and Hugh Garvey and his wife have since become family friends.

Publishing had its own aura, leading me into unexpected places. There was the great Benedictine Abbey of St John by the twin cities of St Paul and Minneapolis: a little-known but splendid example of modern church architecture, the work of the German architect, Bauer. The liturgical scholars there were to be the prime movers of the liturgical changes of Vatican II – men like Godfrey Dieckman, whom I met again at the Council literally dancing in the Piazza di San Pietro when the Decree on the Liturgy was issued. Publishing also took me to Notre Dame University near Chicago, famous unjustly only for its football team. The university press held a leading place in historical scholarship. From there to Harvard where my host was principal of a college and host at the time to T. S. Eliot. The poet seemed totally at home there in a way that could not be said of him in London where he was an exotic despite his complete disguise as a traditional British publisher. He read us some of his poems in that tired, cracked, sonorous voice of his which is their perfect medium.

I came to Georgetown, the Jesuit university near Washington, where I went to sung Mass in an all-black congregation. The only other white was Sergeant Schriver of the Kennedy tribe. My publishing friend there was David McManus, a young innovator who founded the Helicon Press, bilingual in French and an ardent disciple of Teilhard de Chardin. We published Cuénot's standard biography together. He had a couple of young Benedictines staying with him in his Beach House, as he called it. Here the staple delight was soft-shelled crab eaten *de rigeur* off a newspaper. David died young, one of the most brilliant of my publishing friends.

Coming back to base in New York I found an old friend – the indomitable Anne Fremantle – living in a brownstone house off 6th Avenue. Anne, an English peer's daughter, had adopted America, married the chief of the Ouspensky cult – an old Oxford friend – had published several learned anthologies and a well-documented life of Charles de Foucauld. Her home was a haven for English writers passing by, among them Evelyn

Waugh and the ubiquitous Fr D'Arcy. At a party there I ran into Wystan Auden again. I had known him in his undergraduate days: a whimsical, slovenly know-all, but we had parted (as I did with many friends) over the Spanish Civil War. It had put a barricade between us, as also Jacques Maritain and Eric Gill. Roy Campbell with his *Flowering Rifle* (1938) spoke more for my sympathies. But Auden withdrew his neo-Marxist poems in later editions of his work and clearly had changed in his political outlook. It was good to renew an old friendship and I visited him in his Greenwich Village basement where all his temporal needs were supplied by a young Filipino catamite cook. Wystan was to die in the village home he later made his own in Austria. Oxford *retrouvé* was a different Oxford and did not fill his spirit: eternity was lovelier in the little church of Kirchstetten which keeps his grave. The visit to an Americanised Englishman was the last of my trip. I reflected on how little the two sides had blended. Wystan was English to the core despite his contrived and atrocious American accent.

Thinking back about these passing touches with the merest fringes of America, they stay vivid after more than fifty years because they were not part of anything amorphous or anonymous. The United States is a country essentially of people in their own right, as variegated specimens of humanity as can be imagined. There are no stereotypes so there is no blurring of memories, no generalities even now, at this distance in time.

8

Three Spanish Prologues

Could it be that critical moments in one's life, not only trail memories in their wake but are actually preceded by hints, pointers and foreshadowings? At the time of these intimations, they are not recognised as such. At the end of the day they have found their place in a pattern.

I was eighteen when I first beheld the Pyrenees and came to cross them by a high pass on foot, alone. I had no inkling that I was in every sense on the watershed of my life, that I would marry in Spain and go on to spend almost half of my life there. That journey was the first of three prologues, as it were, to a story as yet unfinished.

I had been inspired by an early book of Belloc's on the Pyrenees and was determined to follow his example and cross them on my own. I wrote to him for advice and he invited this young stranger to the Reform Club where he drew sketch-maps of mountain paths. 'And when you come to this place,' said Belloc pointing to a village, 'mention my name at the inn and it may work wonders.' It did, but not in the way which I could conveniently recount to him. 'Ah,' said the innkeeper, 'that charming *German* gentleman.' Belloc, to whom the Franco-Prussian war was like a hair-shirt, would have exploded.

In my ignorance of solitary travel, I had not brought a compass with me. So it was doubtless more my fault than Belloc's that I was soon hopelessly lost on an awesome mountainside. Paths seemed to straggle in all directions, but I came to one running parallel to a stream tumbling down towards a valley, and I decided it must eventually lead to some human habitation. After an hour or so I was rewarded by a blessed sight: a woman leading a donkey laden with firewood. She turned out to be a guardian angel and all smiles. She loaded the donkey with my pack and we talked together with cheerful sign language. Eventually we came to her village. In the setting sun a procession was forming: men carrying candles, women looking down from balconies hung with embroidered bedspreads. A little priest wrapped in a golden chasuble was already under a canopy carrying the Host in a monstrance. I was pushed into the procession and found myself walking with a candle in my hand up a steep cobbled street under a bombardment of flowers from the balconies. It dawned on me that this was the feast of Corpus Christi and the glorious words and rhythms of the *Pange Lingua* came into my head over the stentorian nasal hymns of my companions.

Belloc's book had, after all, sent me to the heart of another country where folklore and a strong undercurrent of mysticism blended as nowhere else in my experience. The weariness in my limbs disappeared and eventually we wound our way back to the *plaza* for a final benediction.

I found a *posada* where two lusty girls made up a large bed for me. They found it a great joke to bounce on the bed and wave their legs. Finally they seemed to take pity on my exhaustion and gave me a huge dish of beans, to be washed down with 'wine that tasted of tar' – Belloc's marvellous poem *Miranda* was here incarnate.

Early next morning I woke from my nirvana and found the little priest sitting on a stone bench with his nose in his breviary. I had little Spanish then, still less any clue to the local *patois*. I fell back on dog-Latin and '*Ubi est hic locus?*' His voluble explanation was lost on me until he too fell back on Latin and I came to realise that I was very far from any place that I had heard of.

Rescue came unexpectedly. I decided to stay another night at the *posada* and a lorry carrying performing dogs, arrived in the afternoon. They gave a fine show to an enchanted audience, seemingly the whole village. One of the terriers was vested as a priest for Mass, complete with a wobbling biretta on his head, and he was witnessing a wedding: the bride in white silk, the bridegroom complete with top hat and spats. The whole joke, repeated several times, was that the bride would constantly interrupt the wedding service by tottering on her hind legs to a nuptial bed where she lay enraptured. The priest had to totter after her several times and bring her back to the ceremony. When at last it was over bride and bridegroom went off to bed together after the priest's final benediction. Loud applause. I doubt if there were any sexual hang-ups in that village.

The two dog-owners were giving performances in two or three villages *en route* to the nearest railhead so I gladly accepted their invitation to join them. We travelled happily for three days: the dogs performed their robust and bawdy roles every evening, and for me a curtain was lifted on a Spain which thus had displayed its unaffected piety and its indelible picaresque character.

The second prologue came about ten years later, in the summer of 1935. I had been at the wedding of two of my best friends. Hemingway was in the air and the young couple had decided on a honeymoon in Pamplona as a sort of re-run of his *Fiesta*. Off they went with their rucksacks after a wedding feast, awash with wine.

To my surprise a telegram from Pamplona arrived some days later, from the wife, beseeching me to go to them, if I could manage it, as soon as possible. To be a gooseberry to a loving couple was not my idea of fun or duty. But the summons was clearly heartfelt. I enlisted a mutual friend in the appropriate person of René Hague and we set off from Boulogne armed with a metre of bread and *saucisson* and a couple of litres of wine, thus alleviating the hardship of *troisième classe* with its remorseless wooden benches.

René Hague was almost in a species of his own, as is each

individual angel, according to Aquinas. He had been at
Ampleforth and Oxford but had left both in circumstances never
explained. There was certainly nothing to his own discredit that
I knew about.

When I temporarily took on the job of a traveller at Sheed &
Ward I visited one day a seedy Catholic secondhand bookseller
in Red Lion Square. The assistant to Mr George Coldwell, the
Dickensian proprietor, was a tall good-looking gaunt young man
suggestive of James Joyce's Daedalus. I was charmed by his
whimsical and detached outlook. It was an instinctive friendship
sealed when a week later he telephoned and asked me to lunch in
his basement flat under the shop. I was sure that he worked for
coolie wages and expected nothing like a feast, but gladly
accepted the invitation.

In his dingy basement room René had a table set with a
tablecloth and napkins, smoked salmon and a bottle of Hock: at
least his week's wages. This began some fifty years of friendship.
Later on René was to marry Joan, a daughter of Eric Gill. Eric at
first disapproved of the young swain who at one point was
minding sheep in the Black Mountains of Wales so as to be near
his beloved Joan, as yet unbetrothed. It seems he would visit Joan
surreptitiously by night on occasion. Once, by mistake, he left
his pocket hairbrush in Joan's room (René was always meticu-
lously well-groomed even in direst poverty). Eric discovered the
brush and there was an almighty row, ending in embraces all
round. Eric not only allowed but insisted on marriage. Joan kept
the hairbrush all her life. René joined his father-in-law to found
Hague & Gill, printers, and produced wonderful work on his
hand press. He was a many-sided genius: a born translator, a
proof reader for the more erudite and complicated productions of
the Cambridge University Press, and best interpreter of the
highly intricate writings of David Jones. He was a very droll and
spontaneous man. No wonder he jumped at the chance of a trip
to Pamplona and indeed he was the ideal companion for that
bizarre event.

Arrived in Pamplona we learnt that the most famous of

matadors, Juan Belmonte, was to have a comeback *corrida*, after some years of absence from the bullring, at nearby Logroño. No sooner said than done, and we were clambering on to the roof of a bus and settling down between trussed sheep, *garafas* of wine and other cargo. It was the cheapest way of travelling.

I remember reading *en route* large election posters calling for support of Gil Robles, the centrist politician. Who could guess that six years later he would be in exile in Lisbon anathematised by the extremists of both right and left, and would be a clandestine contact of mine throughout the Second World War?

Who could guess, too, that Belmonte would in due time become a close friend and 'best man' with others at my wedding in Madrid in 1944? (In Spain a man may invite any number of men friends to be *testigos*, or witnesses, of his marriage. Similarly, the bride chooses *her* men friends and relations.)

Back in Pamplona, we had dinner in the square. With the aid of a napkin and a chair for a bull, René illustrated Belmonte's exploits to an admiring crowd. We had an uproarious dinner with the honeymooners and I could not divine the reason for my urgent summons. I believe I found it by chance the night after. We decided to cross the Pyrenees by the romantic pass of Roncesvalles. It was, incidentally, an appropriate choice because René had just published a memorable translation of the *Chanson de Roland*. A bus took us to where we could walk along the crest of the mountain, shrouded in mist. As evening fell we looked for a lodging and there suddenly appeared a solitary *posada*. A welcoming woman said that she had two bedrooms, one with two single beds and the other *de matrimonio*. The husband quickly claimed the twin-bedded room. 'Not on your life', said Réne, and we both ushered the honeymoon couple to the *cuarto de matrimonio* in some merriment. From the radiant appearance of our honeymooners next morning, I deduced that my mission had been accomplished. This was confirmed by the birth of a lovely child in due time.

★ ★ ★

The third prologue was getting nearer to the main performance. It was in 1938 at the time of the Munich crisis and at the height of the Spanish Civil War. A chance encounter with a friend in a London street led her to ask what I was doing for a summer holiday. I told her that I had no plans. She asked me if I would drive an ambulance, which had been donated by English Catholics, to Burgos, the Spanish Nationalist headquarters. I accepted at once and was delighted to know that my companions would be a family friend, General Pereira (retired but, I suspect, not restrained from observing the situation for military intelligence) and Gabriel Herbert, a friend of debutante dancing days who was a volunteer nurse with the Nationalists, later decorated for valour. (Much later she married Alick Dru of Kierkegaard and St Leonard's Terrace days. Both are now at rest after a life of achievement.)

There were no formalities at the frontier, Irun, but much evidence of war, with shattered buildings and signs of death and shattered lives. We were welcomed at Burgos by the Duchess of Lecera as a delegate of the Red Cross, a diminutive but dynamic lady with cropped hair, in a peaked cap and khaki uniform. She spoke perfect English as does, indeed, most of the Spanish aristocracy. Her somewhat bovine husband was rumoured to be at least the would-be lover of Queen Ena. I was to learn later that, unless they moved in a circumambient atmosphere of scandal, Spanish aristocrats would feel themselves unclothed. Later, in my Madrid days, Rosario Lecera was a loyal friend and a staunch Anglophile. Also there was Pablo Merry del Val, at this time chief liaison officer for the foreign press. He had been my contemporary at Stonyhurst when his father was Spanish Ambassador in London. Pablo was a courteous and dominating personality. He took us to Guernica and patiently explained that the extensive destruction of the main street had been the work of the retreating Reds. Dynamite, not the bombs of the German Condor Legion, was responsible. It was not convincing propaganda and has since been abandoned. 'Bunny' Doble, the actress, was in Burgos waiting for the occasional visits of her lover, Kim Philby, often away as a reporter on various battle fronts. We had many London friends in common and she was good company. I can see her now laughing at my shock at the effect of lemon juice on fresh clams, wriggling and raising their periscopes in apparent surprise.

Such brief escapes from the atmosphere of war were welcome. Otherwise its shadow was all-pervading. Almost everyone was in uniform, the army battledress mingling with the blue shirts and the red berets of the Falange and the *Requetés*.

In the room reserved for the foreign press I found myself glued to the radio, in the company of John Amery and a tall blond young man with a Nazi buttonhole badge, listening to bulletins about the invasion of Czechoslovakia. 'We'll squash those dwarfs flat,' said the Nazi at one point. I glared at him and retorted that in that case he would eventually be squashed flat himself and the swastika banished from the earth.

How could I guess that at the end of the Second World War I would be charged with taking over the German Embassy in Madrid and hoisting the Union Jack on its flagstaff?

John Amery, the only witness to this clash, was silent, withdrawn. He was a romantic figure who had taken up the Nationalist cause, leading him into later and deeper involvement with the Axis as a propagandist in Italy. Years later, in my time at the Madrid embassy, he was tracked down by the Special Branch, taken to England, tried and executed as a traitor. The then Spanish government had granted him Spanish nationality, but this was of no avail. Nor were the efforts of his brother Julian, who gallantly came to Madrid to try and save him. John was misguided but never malevolent and certainly not guilty of any bloody act. He was a victim of hate and hysteria bred by the war. He had shown no sympathy for the Nazi in our brief encounter. His lover's husband had been murdered by the Reds and his consuming passion had been anti-Communist, a passion which he thought his countrymen should share.

This final prologue had introduced me to some of the *dramatis personae* of what was to be the main performance; more important, it brought me direct experience of the intense Nationalist counter-revolutionary spirit which was to pervade Spain well into the Franco era – inward-looking, defiant and full of illusions. I had come to know that battle-scarred road to Burgos without knowing that I would take it again within two years and in very different circumstances.

Looking back now on the 1930s I wonder to what extent I thought of it at the time as a doom-laden decade. Very little, is the mystifying answer. Mystifying because the signs of the times were there for all to see. At home, the foundering of the first-ever Labour government, the slump, the fumbling attempt at a National government, the collapse of the pound and devaluation, the rising tide of unemployment, hunger marches and the unthinkable fact of mutiny in the Navy were somehow accepted as excrescences in an otherwise peaceful and stable situation. Inventiveness in the arts, new writers, new records in sport, new inventions, new discoveries in medicine buoyed up a complacent public. Mr Baldwin, with his reassuring pipe and tweeds, and the media – above all *The Times*– conspired to keep it that way. To that extent I was in the mainstream. Radio was only an incidental channel of information; the invasion of television into every living-room had not yet happened. The world as a global village, where everything is everyone's concern, was to come much later.

The rise of the dictatorships was reported in a muted and distorted fashion: an ugly development, better kept out of sight. Official compliance with broken treaties, near criminal efforts to satisfy Nazi expansionism, by offering to hand over territories that were not ours – such was the coin of our diplomacy. Rearmament, thought Mr Baldwin, would be electorally danger-ous – a prospect which was apparently more alarming to him than any belligerent threat from abroad.

One voice spoke out against government policy and public apathy at every possible opportunity: Winston Churchill ceaselessly exposed Britain's weakness and Germany's growing power. Despite his impressive evidence and formidable eloquence, Churchill was not taken seriously – Parliament ignored him. I remember thinking that he was aggravating great dangers in the very act of denouncing them. The prospect of peace receded with each new barrage of insults and accusations hurled against Hitler. Mine was a view widely shared among many of my friends. We read *Mein Kampf*, published here in 1931, with incredulity, we distrusted the outpourings of the Left Book Club and were as ignorant of German concentration camps and the persecution of the Jews as of the Gulag Archipelago and the enslavement and 'liquidation' of millions of political dissenters in the Soviet Union. Partly because the protagonists of protest against these horrors were, to me, suspect witnesses, partly because my life and work were at full stretch, I did not become involved in these matters.

I befriended such political exiles as came my way. There was Don Sturzo, the diminutive and dynamic founder of the *Partito Popolare*, banned and persecuted by Mussolini. There was a group of centre-party Catholic Germans, companions of Brüning whom Hitler chased from power; and Berdyaev, the Russian Christian philosopher whom I had known in Paris in the 1920s. These solitary prophets and witnesses were welcomed with sympathy as if they had escaped from an earthquake, but an earthquake, we thought, far removed from our island.

The Spanish Civil War brought it nearer. Many saw it as the prelude to the Second World War. In its timing this was true but of its nature it was independent of the Axis. I saw it as something endemic to Spain, the inexorable result of a radically Spanish social sickness. I was confirmed in this view by my later Spanish experience.

But the Civil War certainly had the effect of making the British public 'think European' and awaking it to a menace which it had so largely neglected. I was no pacifist but appeasement to me was not a dirty word and I saw the Munich agreement, 'Peace in our time', as a benediction: as indeed, did the country as a whole.

After a breathing-space of months it was clear that our guarantee to Poland would be honoured, which made war inevitable. Nobody knew what sort of a war it would be; that it would involve the civilian population as much as the armed services, if not more, seemed likely. I had no conception at the time as to how it would involve me personally. I would be on the move, I imagined, though how and where and when was an open question. I went to Fortnum and Mason and invested in a pair of strong brogues and an all-purpose canvas bag.

One night, on the eve of war, I sat at home drinking whisky with Michael Richey, discussing our possible futures. 'Conscientious objection' was plainly inappropriate. But was killing people the only alternative? Michael opted for the most dangerous way out. He went into minesweepers as an ordinary seaman. He was blown up more than once and ended the war with a commission, a reputation as a master navigator and leading the remains of the German fleet into Scapa Flow. God knows how many lives he had saved. After the war he was appointed secretary of the Royal Institute of Navigation and sailed the Atlantic single-handed in his little boat *Jester* eight times. He nearly went down with her in 1989 but survived and built a replica, which has made yet another crossing (in July 1992).

The answer to my own problem came soon: I found myself in Spain on a mission dedicated to preserving its neutrality. Our wonderings over the whisky had come to their own conclusions.

9

Appointment with Madrid

Shortly before the war broke out I had instructions to report to the Ministry of Information. There I was told I was to be 'in charge of Roman Catholic affairs'. This meant, in effect, propaganda to the neutral Catholic countries. It was a vague charter and turned out to be short-lived.

Not long after joining the ministry I happened to run into the head of the Spanish department, Denis Cowan. Quite unexpectedly he invited me to join him on a trip to Madrid by car. It would, he said, give me a chance of assessing Catholic political opinion on the spot for a couple of weeks. He was leaving almost immediately and I accepted his offer straightaway. He was excellent company as we bowled along in a big grey Humber through unoccupied France. I had told my friends that I would be back in no time. But things happened differently. We reached Hendaye by the Spanish frontier and called at the consulate to report. There was an unexpected signal from the Foreign Office instructing Cowan to proceed no further and me to go ahead. It seemed that Cowan was *persona non grata* with the Spanish Government on account of his having served as one of the neutral observers controlling non-intervention during the Civil War. The non-intervention policy had been suspect with the Spanish Nationalists who were convinced that it was a one-side affair, favouring the Republicans. I am sure that Cowan himself was innocent of duplicity but that was irrelevant. We parted with sorrow. It was sad to hear much later that he had been killed in an air-raid.

The road as far as Burgos was familiar – with memories of

Gabriel and the General. But the town itself was transformed. Whereas uniforms had been everywhere and much bustle and movement of men and machines, a sense of urgency, Burgos was now deserted, bereft – like a woman with nothing to do but confront the chores and the tedium of a solitary life.

The long road to Madrid passed through villages shattered by the violence of war. The centre of the city had escaped the sort of devastation that was later to become commonplace all over Europe, but the discernible decay of a long siege, the crumbling outskirts, the scarce traffic and the empty shops all conveyed the sense of a sick city.

I reached the embassy on a Saturday evening, to be told by a friendly porter that the place was virtually closed for the weekend. He advised me to go to the Palace Hotel and to come back on the Monday. The Palace traditionally has something of the panache of London's Savoy but just now was dimly lit and lifeless. A group of journalists was predictably to be found in the bar but I had no inclination to mix with them, as I had no identity at this time, no reason for being there that I cared to reveal. A new sort of loneliness had been thrust upon me. I thought this would last, perhaps, for a week and I would go home, but I already had an inexplicable sense of belonging to the scene.

My first contact at the embassy was Bernard Malley, a stooping scholarly figure in his forties. He had lived in Spain for most of his adult life and was a teacher of English at a school in the Escorial when the Civil War broke out. The Spanish Government had given free reign to violence and particularly to religious persecution. The monks of the Escorial, if fortunate, were on holiday. Bernard had taken refuge in the British Embassy. There his exceptional knowledge of Spanish life and the language was recognised and he eventually joined the staff of Sir Robert Hodgson, the British agent in Burgos before the diplomatic recognition of General Franco's regime in February 1939. As soon as the embassy had been re-established in Madrid he went there and became the equivalent of an Oriental secretary: an unfailing source of information and wisdom for the transient diplomats and attachés.

As for myself, I could not have found anyone better informed precisely about the area which concerned me: Catholic opinion on the war in lay and clerical circles and its influence on the Spanish Government. That was my brief from the Ministry of Information.

Don Bernardo (as he was known through the embassy and beyond) always spoke in the lowered tones normally reserved for sacristans. He was a fervent Catholic but would chuckle over ecclesiastical scandals. He was happier in two-star rather than five-star circles, with captains rather than higher ranks, with parochial clergy rather than bishops. Thus he gleaned information and exercised influence in areas seldom reached by the career diplomats. We were to become close colleagues in the years that followed. In Bernard Malley I not only found a friend but struck a mine of information which saved me weeks of study and seemed to make it possible to return at once to London with my brief accomplished.

Things turned out quite differently. Hardly had a week gone by when the ambassador – Sir Samuel Hoare – told me that he had 'made all arrangements' for me to join his staff as Press Attaché with the rank of First Secretary; my job would be largely of my own making. Moreover, my responsibility would be to him, not to the Ministry of Information. I protested my inadequacy and lack of experience, but all objections were brushed aside. Perhaps he thought that the job would be short-lived anyway, since he was very fearful of a German invasion at that time.

Meeting the mandarins of the Chancery was a chilling experience. They were at first fish-eyed, aloof and polite to this foreign body thrust into their midst. The Service, Economic and Commercial attachés were more welcoming. The secret services, not quite sure whether I belonged to one branch or other, were cautiously friendly. The cypher-room girls, high-born and high-spirited, were intrigued, but then they were used to being intrigued.

Altogether I soon realised that I was joining a close-knit family of many talents and many tensions. We were welded into friendship by a virtual isolation from the outside world.

An annexe of the embassy harboured the secret services, a mixed bag: smooth SIS professionals mixed with rather jolly and cynical fruit shippers from Valencia, later joined by SOE, mainly young merchant bankers from the City. They were a friendly lot but I could never quite make out what they were achieving. They would ply me with questions as time went on and I gained their confidence. I was sometimes struck by the ingenuous character of their enquiries. SOE – the merchant bankers – were apparently making contingent plans in the event of a German invasion. I chose not to take the diplomatic train as a way out but to go underground in Spain. The merchant bankers suggested that I lie low in a monastery for a spell. I do not think that they had any contact with any religious community, or with much else for that matter.

The SIS produced fleeting visitors from time to time: a picture dealer and specialist in Spanish art, a schoolmaster claiming to be an expert on Gracian, a hero from Franco's side in the Civil War (who was promptly sent off by an indignant ambassador), a ballistics expert, Major Pollard, who had helped to fly Franco from the Canaries to Morocco at the outset of the Civil War. They were all colourful characters but, it seemed to me, without a role of much importance.

The film star, Leslie Howard, was another reputedly on a highly secret mission. I arranged a press conference for him and a luncheon for show business people and the media. He made an admirable speech with an impeccable Spanish accent which he had learnt by heart in a couple of hours. He hardly surfaced for the next twenty-four hours and I had to cancel a number of social engagements. He kept a lengthy one himself, however, with the manicurist of his hotel whom, to my embarrassment, he even smuggled on to his train back to Lisbon. From there he wrote me a charming letter of thanks, '... for everything ... It seems to me you were the best of the bunch.' He was killed when his plane was shot down over the French coast on the way home, the only one on that regular run to London to meet that fate. I agree with those who say that the German fighters went out in force because Churchill was reported to be on board. It so happened that Leslie Howard's manager had a striking resemblance to the Prime Minister and Lisbon airport was well supplied with German spies.

A highly effective department, working on its own, was responsible for the reception and safe shipment through Spain to Gibraltar of escaped prisoners of war and other military personnel who managed to evade the occupying army. A network of escape routes from northern France down to the frontier serviced by gallant men and women – mostly French – was responsible for the transit of some hundreds of Allied troops and airmen.

The heads of the family were, of course, the ambassador and the minister. The latter, Arthur Yencken, was a small, highly polished and anglicised Australian whose previous post had been Berlin. He had won an MC in the Great War and was tough, laconic, witty and sometimes rather wild. He ruled that variegated collection of men and women with deceptive ease and was very much in his element on the diplomatic cocktail circuit.

A few months after my arrival he sent his wife and children to their Australian home in view of the German threat of invasion, and invited me to share his house. I came to value his trust and companionship enormously. 'One of your many jobs here will be to keep Sam from doing a bunk,' he told me at one of our first talks. It took me some time to see what he meant.

The comment that Samuel Hoare was descended from a long line of maiden aunts is attributed to Winston Churchill. A certain testiness in discussion was linked to a tidiness in appearance and ideas. He was abstemious himself and somewhat mean to others in matters of food and drink. There was a lack of generosity in small gestures towards subordinates, something I experienced a few years later when I got married in 1944. For the sake of the embassy I hid from view the shoddy present he produced for my wedding, coming as it did from my chief of four years and a principal participant at the ceremony. He led my bride to the altar, a magnanimous gesture in all the circumstances. As they went up the isle he whispered to her, 'My father would turn in his grave if he saw me doing this.'

Not without reason Sir Samuel was extremely nervous about his personal safety. He was shadowed by a stalwart from Special Branch on his daily walk to the embassy. He was in fact ill at ease in Spanish society and I came to appreciate Yencken's injunction. His alienation stemmed from an indelible insularity reinforced by his inbred Anglo-Catholic convictions. All this distanced him from the Latin temperament. It also put a barrier between him and the United States ambassador. Carlton Hayes was a professor of Columbia University, a specialist in Spanish sixteenth-century history, a devout Catholic and an admirer of Isabella, the great queen of the Conquest. As regards Franco, what Samuel Hoare saw as an arrogant upstart regime, Carlton Hayes would have seen as a return to the spirit of the sixteenth century. The lack of understanding between the British and United States embassies struck me as absurd and I did my best to bridge the gap at my own level, forming valued friendships with the Americans.

Samuel Hoare's personal failings were largely overcome by his own dynamisn. He was absorbed in his station and its duties, restlessly determined to advance or initiate whatever might help in his mission. He had, after all, occupied almost every high Cabinet office before he came to Madrid and he gave to the post and the embassy an *éclat* and a significance all its own.

He was not, however, an infallible judge of character and opportunity. When he came to Madrid the Spanish Minister of Foreign Affairs was General Beigbeder, a genial soldier with a North African background. He had an English mistress and bought his hats at Lock's. Although it was unlikely that Samuel

Hoare would follow his example in such matters, the ambassador seemed to find some reassurance in the general's preferences, as he also did in the general's deep distrust of the Falangist elements in the Spanish Government.

But one fine day General Beigbeder found himself dismissed, for no apparent reason. His place was taken by Ramon Serrano Suñer, brother-in-law of General Franco and virtually the leader of the Falange. It was 18 October 1940. On that morning, the ambassador greeted me at our customary daily session with a grim face: 'Tom, I think my mission to Spain is finished.' I told him that, in my view, it was just about to begin. I explained that he would no longer be facing a dummy figure at the ministry but the man closest of all to General Franco's mind and policies: it was a wonderful opportunity to review and renew Anglo-Spanish relations. The ambassador was not convinced: the new minister was his opposite in every way, a passionate National-Catholic, an eloquent rabble-rouser, a clever lawyer and a flamboyant womaniser. Serrano Suñer was physically and mentally courageous and avowedly pro-German. Sam must have been sorely tempted, in Yencken's phrase, 'to do a bunk' from such a figure, especially as he was the harbinger of increased German pressure if not of actual invasion.

I had formed a different opinion of Serrano Suñer: he was too much of a patriotic Spaniard to be the tool of another country. His pro-German feelings sprang from his passionate hatred of Soviet Communism with the horror it had brought to his own country, including the death of his two brothers. Subsequent records go to show that if any single man in the Spanish Government at that time was a major influence in keeping Spain out of the war and preventing the passage of German troops through to Gibraltar that man was Serrano Suñer. He had no reason to love Britain, he had been refused asylum by our embassy when he and his kind were being hunted down in Madrid by the local *chekas* and shot out of hand in the early days of terror. Clearly at that time, the early days of the Civil War, the embassy had no grasp of what was happening. I was told that the, then, *chargé d'Affaires* would even drive down to his morning golf without apparently taking account of corpses scattered along his route. Why did almost every embassy except the British offer sanctuary to those who were in danger of their lives simply because of their political opinions, their wealth or their religion?

The Royal Navy seemed to have its own view about the refugees and took aboard its destroyers public figures in danger of the fanatical gunmen of the so-called government; my wife-to-be and her family were among those rescued and shipped to France.

The normal duties and opportunities of a press attaché were neither relevant nor practicable in the Franco dictatorship. There was no press open to Allied news, there were no editorial policies to discuss and possibly influence. The entire press was under the direction of an under-secretary and a director-general of the Falange party. These two appointed and dismissed editors, columnists and correspondents and issued minute instructions on how to treat the news each day. After a time I managed to suborn the official who passed on these instructions and I received a copy of them every day, at least giving me some insight into the Spanish Government's preoccupations. The editors and principal columnists were all in the pay of the German press attaché, Herr Lazar, and no money in the world could have turned them. Happily, the Spaniards on the whole are not addicted to the press and in any case quite cynical about its views. I doubt, therefore, whether the German occupation of the media had much practical effect.

To some extent this put a premium on the embassy bulletin which I issued every day, taken from a special wireless service from London. Every evening a continuously moving queue of 1,000 or so would shuffle past the porter's lodge of my office and take away a handful for local distribution. The men were mainly from the poorer quarters of the city and were in sharp contrast to the elegant district where my office was installed. Sometimes the queue reached right around the block.

Spanish officials protested at my 'Red propaganda' but could find nothing to justify the charge. I was not helped, however, by the fact that the office apparently lay on the route from one detention camp to another. Lorry-loads of prisoners of war on forced labour would greet the bulletin queue with cheerful shouts, clenched fists and cries of '*Viva Inglaterra*'.

I could not help reflecting that this luckless mass of men would quickly stifle their *vivas* if they knew what British policy was: to keep Spain neutral by doing nothing to disturb Franco's hold on the country and when possible to aid it economically. To prevent the Germans marching through to attack Gibraltar was our major objective. (The Duke of Alba – General Franco's ambassador in London – would say that Churchill, lunching at his embassy, had promised Gibraltar to Spain in return for its neutrality but, needless to say, this was later disavowed by the Foreign Office, after the war.)

It is of course heartening to a government agent of any kind when he finds that the official policy which it is his job to project is totally congenial with his personal opinions. In my case I hoped and worked for Spanish neutrality with a will. I had long since come to the conclusion that, contrary to the general view in Britain, the Spanish Civil War was not by design a rehearsal for the Second World War, thus linking Franco ineluctably with the Axis, but was a phenomenon specifically of Spanish political history. It would have happened regardless of any wider European situation. That the Axis supported The Movement, as it was called, is undeniable; also undeniable is the fact that the Soviets and world Communism had supported the Republican government in the Civil War. But had these giants been off the scene, the fatal clash in Spain itself would still have come about. When King Alfonso went into exile in 1931 'to avoid bloodshed', the knives were already sharpening – well ahead of Hitler's power and designs.

In conversation with Spanish friends one frequently met the phrase 'our war' as opposed to 'your war'. At first it shocked me and appeared unrealistic and totally disproportionate. But I came to realise that for the Spaniards 'our war' was a special tragedy – small, of course, compared with that of Europe but just as intense and personally more traumatic: few families were without their once-loved dead. In the Second World War, the Spaniards were spectators and it suited Allied policy to keep them so. But there was trouble on our own propaganda front. The Foreign Office stoutly supported the embassy but the BBC took its own line. Being partly staffed with Spanish exiles and academics of Republican sympathies, it had a high old time lambasting Franco and the Falangists, suggesting to the Republicans that they had lost a battle but not the war, and that their fortunes would change with an Allied victory.

The more I penetrated Spanish life, the more I came to realise that it had a code, customs, and a charisma exclusively its own. A foreigner could love or hate it: he could not be indifferent. My penetration into that life was unexpected and far-reaching beyond imagining. In my first weeks at the embassy – unknown and unknowing – I often had only myself for company. One day I settled for lunch in a *taberna* which had an inviting look and sat in a corner with *The Times* for company. The only other occupants of the place filled a long table, being bent it would seem on some celebration. I took them to be stage or literary people of some sort: two of them being lovely women, the assortment of males might be anything from bullfighters to writers – and indeed proved to be so.

One of their number suddenly detached himself from their table and came across to me politely enquiring in Hollywood English who I was and so on. I explained briefly and was invited to join his friends. It proved to be an entry into a section of Madrid life which no diplomatic channel could ever offer.

One of the subtler specialities of Spanish life is the *tertulia* – a self-constituted, self-perpetuating group of men of shared views and interests, whether political or professorial, which meets regularly in a cafe or *taberna* for companionable talk. It has the characteristics of a London club in miniature: exclusive and inward-looking. As with a London club, people do not join a *tertulia* just because they want to but because they are elected or invited to join by its members.

So, suddenly, I was admitted to a *tertulia*, at that time hardly knowing its nature and least of all the character of this particular one. If it called itself anything it was the *tertulia* of the Golden Lion, an ancient café in the heart of Madrid. I soon came to realise that this *tertulia* was, in its way, unique. The luncheon turned out to be a by-product: the main business was in the Lion after dinner. There was a lot of desultory chat, a good deal of badinage and occasional intense argument. Politics hardly came into it. The wounds of war were so recent, the pursuits of peace had at long last to be given root-room.

My memory of the *tertulia* after some fifty years is still vivid. It slightly changed its composition from night to night but the regulars were in the majority – vivid personalities undimmed by time. The most loquacious was Antonio Cañabate, the leading bullfight critic of the day, a lank owl-like character, droll and undomesticated. The portentous presence of Eugenio d'Ors, the Catalan poet and critic, could be guaranteed; so too could the equally imposing Ignacio Zuloaga, the Basque painter. Domingo Ortega and Juan Belmonte, the great bullfighters, respectively from Old Castille and Andalusia, came often. Ortega was then at the height of his powers, Belmonte was retired and relaxed. There was Sebastian Miranda, an eccentric sculptor who was later to play a decisive part in my life; Eusebio Oliver, an ascetic doctor of some renown; 'El Gordo', an antiquarian bookseller who lived up to his name; Edgar Neville, the Spanish film producer from Hollywood, who had befriended me at lunch; Emilion Garcia Gomez, a learned Arabist. There were many others: a bull-breeder from Salamanca, a chemist, a publisher. Occasionally

wives and mistresses drifted in. Besides these nightly meetings in
the café, this *tertulia* jointly owned a box in the bullring and the
crowd would turn its head there for some sign of approval of one
act or another in the ritual of the *corrida*.

Those evenings at the Golden Lion became a matter of habit;
they were convivial but with the austerity that underlies much of
Spanish life. Imperceptibly I was discovering that life, its
language and lore. I had struck a rich vein of the essential Spain
– the permanent *país* – distinct from the polarised passions of the
Civil War – which, however, were still far from extinguished.

By the end of the Civil War and well into my first year in Madrid,
Spain had been a country occupied by its own army and largely
administered by the Falange party. General Franco had made an
amalgam of these two disparate bodies with a third, the
traditionalist *Requetes*, and called it The Movement. He would on
occasion symbolise this by sporting the red beret of the *Requetes*,
the blue shirt of the Falange and his general's uniform. As one
came closer to the scene one could see the rifts and divisions in
the all-embracing Movement. The army was often at odds with
the Falange and the latter was divided against itself.

The Falange's young aristocratic founder, José Antonio Primo
de Rivera, had been shot by the Reds in prison at the outbreak of
the Civil War. The leadership and even the role of the party were
in dispute. Unconditional loyalty to Franco was the predominant
characteristic, but some of the 'old shirts', the original Falangists,
saw National Socialism as the necessary reward of a military
victory. This was anathema to the army. Franco had dealt
toughly with the first signs of revolt: by the firing squad or
imprisonment.

Among those who survived, I met a preposterous character,
one Señor de Velasco, who purported to be in the counsels of
Serrano Suñer the foreign minister at the time. According to de
Velasco, Suñer mistrusted the Anglophile tendency of Spain's

ambassador in London and wanted a man of his own on the spot to assess British morale and the British capability for continuing the struggle – in other words his personal spy. On a visit to my suite at Gaylords Hotel in Madrid, de Velasco's project was explained to me with a wealth of colourful detail about himself, how he had been under sentence of death and reprieved by Franco, how he had been the champion masturbator of the military prison, how he was a deadly shot. To prove this last he suddenly produced a pistol with a silencer and sent a bullet whizzing past my left ear. It seemed to be his way of sealing a bond. Gaylords had been the Soviet headquarters in the Civil War and perhaps more than one bullet had lodged in the elegant moulding round the ceiling.

Anyway, to have a spy easy to tail might lead to others and de Velasco's idea was welcomed by MI5. It ended in fiasco: de Velasco, on arrival, immediately contacted the London correspondent of Spain's leading paper and got him into deepest trouble. Never a spy in my view, and indeed sometimes a helpful reporter of British war moves, the correspondent was saved from execution through the intervention of the Duke of Alba with Churchill and packed off to Spain. I never saw de Velasco again and wonder what nonsense he must have brought back to Serrano Suñer.

When I first arrived in Madrid the youngest member of the Government was Pedro Gamero del Castillo. It so happened that we both lodged at Gaylords and often dined alone at separate tables. After a week or so of this, on an impulse, I passed my card to him and suggested taking coffee together. He immediately agreed and a friendship was formed between us which lasted until his death from cancer long after the war. He was an Andalusian and had been civil governor of Seville until his promotion to Minister without Portfolio at the age of thirty-six. He was certainly striking in appearance: tall, with a high forehead and deep-set piercing brown eyes and an enormous smile. I realised that I was confronted with a man of outstanding intelligence. He was loosely Falangist, a radical idealist, far more concerned for justice and peace in his own country than with the world war. But without betraying secrets he was able to convey to me which members of the government were good neutralists and which were all for Spain's entry into the war and a German victory. But above all Pedro gave me some insight into the causes of the Civil War: how it was to be young and hopeful and desperate under the moribund monarchy, how the Republic foundered in anarchy – and how helpless an adult Catholic could feel in the stifling atmosphere of the Spanish Church of the time.

The wide spectrum – from the mountebanks to the mystics of Falangism – included many pig-headed officials in my particular field, the media. Officially I had charge of the press offices in Barcelona, Lisbon and Tangier, but after visits to them all, I decided that this made no sense. Their problems were less pressing than mine, they were in competent and experienced hands: Paul Dorchy at Barcelona was a brash and robust young man who rightly regarded his duties as being adaptable to circumstances rather than what London would regard as proper to a press office. Not the least of his exploits was to smuggle the future Belgian Prime Minister, Henri Spaak, across the Pyrenees in the boot of his car.

His opposite number in Lisbon, Marcus Cheke, was opposite in every sense. He was aloof and aristocratic in manner. He was a serious student of Portuguese history and the author of a book on Pombal. He was on the friendliest terms with Anglophile politicians and newspaper proprietors. I could not have wished for a more helpful colleague. Fittingly he ended his career after the war as vice-marshal of the Diplomatic Corps.

My visits to Lisbon were infrequent and their usefulness lay in the chance it gave me to make contact with monarchist and other non-Communist exiled politicians such as Gil Robles and Saenz-Rodriquez. A mild form of wishful-thinking conspiracy was kindled occasionally by lengthy luncheons but I learnt to expect nothing by way of action. The court of Juan Alfonso, pretender to the throne in remote Estoril, had an Oriental immobility about it.

The contrast between Madrid and Lisbon was total. Portugal was proud of being 'Britain's oldest ally' and one was popular almost everywhere. The country had been at peace with itself under Salazar's paternal dictatorship. It was an incongruous outpost of prosperity in stricken Europe.

Tangier, again, was different. Two retired colonels ran the Information Office. They had little to do and seemed to be doing it very well. I left them in peace in that turbulent city. Charlie's Bar – of international repute – was a more fruitful source of information. Charlie was reputedly a Cambridge graduate, a tall, elegant, dark-skinned African. Clearly he delighted in his somewhat *louche* and sinister customers. 'Everything happens here,' he told me, 'if you bring your wife I will have to charge you corkage.' His quip was unconsciously ironic as I had no wife and the prospect of having one had suddenly vanished when I had passed through Gibraltar on the previous day.

At the Rock Hotel there, turned into an officers' mess, I had run into an old school-friend whom I had not seen for years and I enquired casually after his brother. 'Oh, don't you know?' he answered on a slightly elated note, 'he's going to marry X' (the name was of public interest and I might be expected to know it). 'Oh ... I thought *I* was!' came unbidden from my stupefied brain. This was the only news of X that had reached me in weeks. I had blamed the wartime posts and her hard work as a VAD. She had been a constant presence in my life in the past three years. My departure from London had been too sudden for any solemn undertaking about the future, but we had parted with mutual trust. For my part this protected me, in some measure, from succumbing to all the feminine enchantment that came my way in Madrid. Any budding affair of the heart had been checked by what seemed a beckoning purpose in my life. Suddenly all of this vanished: no presence, no trust, no discernible purpose. It would take a long time for this to be changed from a vacuum to a new vision, free from the bondage and illusion of years.

The odds against that meeting in Gibraltar were almost infinite, but all the same it happened. The single moment left an indelible mark. Not for the first time I had come to see a coincidence as a providential pointer. This was in December 1940. I went back to a Madrid that was more than ever fearful of the immediate future. German pressure on Spain to join the Axis was intensified, the triumphalist speeches of General Franco and his ministers became more strident and the hostile attitude of minor functionaries more galling.

Certainly everything seemed to be stacked against us in Madrid if one's views were based on the endless ructions with Spanish officialdom and on the continued German initiatives and triumphs on various fronts. But I had grown sceptical about official attitudes and the wisdom of statesmen. I was sustained by two gut convictions: first, that the Spaniards would not get themselves embroiled in the war on any account and, second, that an Allied victory was sure to come in the long run. There was no logic leading up to these conclusions, they were to me like articles of faith transferred into the secular world and they sustained me as might the Apostles' Creed in other connections.

It had struck me, after meeting so many Spanish officials at close quarters, that they were playing at being Falangists and Fascists: the role was not in the Spanish nature. It was fashionable, of course, but that is to say that it was ephemeral. I could not believe that the dummy deputies in the Cortes, the ministers and undersecretaries, would be permanently comfortable in their midnight-blue shirts, white coats and black trousers. Spain could never be itself in those clothes. Some years later my view was confirmed when I read a jotting by that wise and witty and ill-starred man, Manuel Azaña, the last president of the Republic.

Writing in 1933, halfway between the fall of the monarchy and the outbreak of the Civil War, his *Notebook* records:

There are, or could be, as many Fascists as you like in Spain. But there will never be a Fascist regime. If sheer force overcomes the Republic, the country will fall back into a military and ecclesiastical dictatorship of the traditional kind, despite all decrees and slogans to the contrary. Military sashes, clerical cassocks, military parades and pious processions to the *Virgen del Pilar*. In that sense the country has nothing else to offer.

It is almost a photographic vision of Franco's rule. The country was indeed full of Falangists, and they tended to get the best jobs, but there were cracks in the scenario through which one could see Azaña's vision. That vision became fully realised by the end of the Spanish Civil War with General Franco supreme, and lasted until his death and the creation of a constitutional monarchy.

Pressure on the embassy increased in 1941 with the collapse of France and the arrival of the Germans on the Spanish frontier. They made the most of it by sending in massed bands of their regiments who stamped their way down Madrid's main avenue playing national music. Himmler came too – to strengthen the ties of the Gestapo with the Spanish secret service. A special bullfight was laid on for them with the most famous *toreros* of the day. Gerry Young, who was then the ambassador's private secretary, and I decided to go along. We calculated that the German national anthem would be played at the end of the *corrida* and planned to leave before the last bull. Unfortunately for us the band struck up with *Deutschland über Alles* halfway through and the vast crowd rose to its feet with upraised arms in salute. I agreed with Gerry that we could not stand up, so we continued to sit. There was fierce protestation all round but we explained that being *Ingleses* we could do no other. Our immediate neighbours agreed but the vast majority – out of earshot – took up an awesome roar. In no time two sturdy blond giants who identified themselves as Gestapo sought to arrest us. To my relief I saw a pair of the *Guardia Civil* climbing up the terrace towards us and told the Germans that I was under Spanish arrest, which soon proved to be the case. We were marched off to the yard where the dead bulls are dragged off by teams of mules and advised by a sympathetic *capitán* not to move until everything was over and the crowd had dispersed.

It was chilling experience in many ways: the mass hysteria, the contact with the ubiquitous Gestapo and, finally, the less than cordial reception we received from our own Samuel Hoare: '... irresponsible ... endangering my mission ... you might have been lynched or kidnapped by the Gestapo ...' Years later in London Roy Campbell told me that he had been at that famous bullfight on the far side of the ring and seen it all without knowing who or what was involved. 'You should have been recommended for the VC,' he growled over his beer.

★   ★   ★

A still centre in a stormy world was the British Institute – personified in Professor Walter Starkie, paradoxically the most Irish of the Irish. He was an amazing man, to use his favourite adjective. Before the war and whenever he could get away from his chair at Trinity College, Dublin, he had travelled all over Spain, mainly with the gypsies and earning his keep with his fiddle.

I think it was Lord Lloyd, then head of the British Council, who made this imaginative appointment. For how could official Spain ever say that Starkie was *persona non grata?* He knew more about the country, its literature and folklore than most Spaniards, its politics had never concerned him and he could hardly be suspected of being a British agent.

The Institute stood apart from the embassy, and was itself an embassy to the survivors of Spain's intellectual eclipse. Any evening one could count on finding there a great novelist such as Pio Baroja, a rising star like José Camilo Cela (since then a Nobel prizewinner), that prince of essayists, Azorin, composers like Rodrigo. These quiet assemblies in Starkie's gloomy head-quarters at the time were by no means peninsular in outlook. True, the England which they revered was more of Dickens than of Churchill: but this was authentic Spain in touch with an authentic England.

Inevitably I and Starkie came to be dubbed Don Quixote and Sancho Panza. I was then as tall and lean as a pole and Starkie's height roughly equalled his girth. We were able to travel together on occasion. Once we went to Gibraltar at the invitation of Captain 'Hooky' Holland, Commander of the *Ark Royal*. Starkie's violin concert in the great hangar below deck of that famous aircraft carrier was unforgettable, with the crew crouched or suspended among the overhanging girders giving thunderous applause. 'Hooky' accepted Starkie's invitation to come, strictly *incognito*, to Madrid for a flamenco party. Starkie's mausoleum-cum-house was lit with candles. He had collected gypsies from who knows where plus the wide variety of his friendship. The flamenco singing and dancing went on until the small hours. Suddenly I heard Starkie announce a toast – 'to my most honoured guest Captain Holland of the *Ark Royal*'. It was a horrifying and dangerous breach of security. I devoutly hoped that our naval attaché would not come to hear of it, still less his German counterpart.

Starkie also did a great deal to keep the small British colony in good heart: the men and women who had lived through the Civil War, keeping their banks and other businesses open. Embassies tend to be stand-offish towards their local nationals and ours was no exception, absurd though this was in the circumstances. Samuel Hoare did little more than tolerate Starkie – his complete opposite in every way. Starkie maintained that he was shabbily treated by the British Council at the end of the war; he left behind him a thriving institute which now has a school of more than 1,000 students.

There can be no doubt that my being a Catholic and moreover connected with Catholic publishing and journalism greatly helped in making friendly contact with like-minded men. For instance, there were many who had been connected with *El Debate* – the Catholic centre paper during the Republic. It could not survive or abide the advent of left-wing censorship and propaganda before the outbreak of the Civil War and was finally suppressed. After the war it would not accept the strict control of the Franco government and never reappeared.

By then some of its writers had been murdered by the Reds, some were in exile and a few – qualified lawyers and so on – had found other means of survival in poverty-stricken Madrid. Many became friends: their exceptional knowledge of the personalities in power all helped me to find my way in otherwise disheartening circumstances. I am thinking especially of men like Francisco de Luis – 'Paco' – a squat square-headed father of a *familia numerosa* from Aragon, a land famous for the obstinacy and honesty of its sons. He had been at the head of *El Debate* and now he was powerless in the press and was building a new career. Another friend was Alberto Martin Artajo who was head of *El Debate*'s holding company: *Editorial Catolica*. He was rather too sympathetic to the Franco regime for the likes of his former colleagues but by no means a man of The Movement and I found him a congenial companion.

Anglophile Madrid – a mixture of academics and aristocrats – came to my office every week to invitation showings of documentaries and scarcely veiled propaganda films such as *In Which We Serve*. My big room was turned into a theatre seating up to 150 or so and, as we worked through our lists, there was a very ready response, encouraged perhaps by a buffet which I laid on. There was virtually no bread in Madrid in my first year, but there were ample supplies from Gibraltar, channelled through the admirable Mrs Taylor, owner of the 'we-never-closed' Embassy Bar, a well known English establishment who supplied good sandwiches for my guests. Whatever their station they were as needy as the next one in those days. Those cinema sessions were little oases of optimism in the darkest times of the war.

Certainly there was nothing of comfort in the news for a very long time, nothing to suggest that Germany's strength and achievement could ever be brought to dust. The German-dominated press was triumphant. The Spanish military men and the Falangist party were openly predicting German victory. But there was a quiet undercurrent of opinion in the opposite sense. There was the innate confidence of the old monarchists that

Britain was unconquerable, the shrewd reckoning in the same sense of journalists and intellectuals who had lost their jobs through Franco's totalitarian rule. The Church needed no reminding of the pagan spirit of Nazi Germany and the workers had a blind faith in Britain.

I decided to produce a special news bulletin for the latter, purporting to come from the Spanish Democratic Union – which never existed – and packets of this sheet, suitably disguised as to type and paper used, were left regularly with contacts on the outskirts of Madrid. The secret sympathisers could never have formed any sort of effective opposition or resistance but morale was being kept up.

There were some setbacks of course. One day it occurred to me that my friend the poet Roy Campbell would be an invaluable agent in case of a German invasion. He was an old soldier; with his family he had sunk entirely into a Spanish background. He lived under the walls of Toledo and made a living in the mule trade between Toldeo and Talavera. I drove down to see him, found him more than eager to have an active part in the war, and that he would be an agent in place seemed a fine idea to both of us. Unfortunately he chose to celebrate this appointment with friends in a café that night – letting it be known that he had been accepted into the British secret service. I had to disown him next day, to my chagrin.

The Spanish Government's embarrassment at being supportive of a Germany which had strong ties with the Soviet Union (Spain's arch-enemy) had come abruptly to an end with Hitler's invasion of Russia in June 1941. Britain became overnight the ally of Spain's arch-enemy. Orchestrated attacks on the embassy followed, with so-called students throwing stones. Our police protection was minimal, the ambassador made official protests in person to Serrano Suñer and General Franco and the incidents were passed over with apologies. They seemed, if anything, to attract the sympathy of the ordinary *madrileño* who had had his fill of violent disorder and was prompted by an innate courtesy to protest against such blatantly bad manners.

So far as I was concerned I found kindness and understanding and sometimes rather embarrassing sympathy on every side. At one dinner party my host, a distinguished lawyer, commiserated with me at the disappearance of the British way of life – which he admired so much – that must follow our defeat. This was too much for another guest, a large contractor and civil engineer: 'Nonsense, the English are going to win the war.'

'What makes you think so?' enquired our host.

'*Porque los Ingleses son mucho mas brutos que los Alemanes.*' (Because they are much more ruthless than the Germans.)

This was typical talk in 1941.

★ ★ ★

Three years went by: momentous all over Europe. The Spain that I had come into was being transformed, power was passing to the new technocrats, Falangism was on the way out, its fiery foreign minister, Serrano Suñer, had been replaced by the cautious and courteous General Jordana. General Franco remained aloof, enigmatic, in total control.

In 1943, some of the great intellectual figures from Republic times returned from exile. The philosopher, Ortega y Gasset, author of *The Revolt of the Masses* and so much else, could once more pack a theatre with a lecture, although he was denied his chair at the university. But a number of historians, scientists and other intellectuals who had been suspected of liberalism by both sides – and therefore of being dangerous elements in society – quietly took up their academic positions again. The greatest of all in public esteem and affection was Dr Gregorio Marañon. He represented a *via media* in all things, a position which his compatriots admired but seldom took. It had been in his consulting room back in 1931 that the transfer from Monarchy to Republic had taken place. He became known as 'the midwife of the Republic'.

San Sebastian, 1945. With three great Spaniards: (from left) *José Ortega y Gasset (philosopher); myself; Ignacio Zuloaga (painter); my father-in-law, Gregorio Marañon (physician)*

Toledo, 1973. De Gaulle, flanked by myself and my sisters-in-law, Patricia Marañon (left), and Carmen Araoz with Mabél (right)

Married in Madrid, 1944: (opposite) Samuel Hoare, British Ambassador, accompanies Mabél to our wedding; (above) Mabél and I leave the church of San Jeronimo; (below) Juan Belmonte, bullfighter, signs the register

Four Old Burgundians: (from top, clockwise) *Arthur Ransome; Douglas Jerrold; Felix Aylmer; Daniel Macmillan with Stanley Morison. Pen-and-ink studies by Robert Lutyens (1962)*

Marañon had continued with his hospital work in Madrid for the first six months of the Civil War, with two daughters as voluntary nurses, until the socialist government could no longer guarantee his safety from its extremists. A British destroyer took the family to France. He lived in Paris through four years of exile, excoriated by both sides in the conflict. It was late in 1943 that word went round, 'Marañon is back', the first hint of some return to normality. His time in Paris had not been wasted; he wrote a compendious *Dictionary of Diagnosis* which has become an indispensable work of reference for doctors in Spain and Latin America. He also continued with his seminal studies in sixteenth-century Spanish history. Meanwhile his son-in-law, returning before him, had restored his beloved home outside Toledo, wrecked in the war. It had been built by the Franciscans about 1620 but had fallen into decay. Marañon bought it in 1921 and created a veritable haven for his family and countless friends.

Among these was Sebastian Miranda, the droll sculptor of my *tertulia*. 'Marañon is back and you must meet him,' he announced one day. He arranged for us to drive down one Sunday afternoon for the leisurely *sobre-mesa* customary on festive occasions, when brandy and *anis* would glint in the sun alongside the coffee-cups. Miranda always seemed to include some unexpected incident in his daily life and our drive down to Toledo was no exception. Halfway down we were confronted by a long goods train athwart a level-crossing, like a sleeping crocodile on a river bed, with no sign of movement. 'Leave it to me,' said Miranda, and I saw him approach the driver and point to my car flying its large Union Jack. In no time the train was broken in two and we passed through, with much banging of buffers as the train closed behind us. 'What did you say?' I asked. 'I said you were the British ambassador on urgent business.' We proceeded to a restaurant outside Toledo where I noticed a distinguished figure whom I took to be an Anglican parson because he could not possibly be anything else. We enjoyed our lunch but the solitary figure was obviously waiting for his host. Suddenly the door opened and a very flustered Samuel Hoare burst in. 'I'm sorry, my dear bishop, but I was held up by goods train at a level-crossing. My chauffeur explained that I was the British ambassador but was told that he had already passed through and that the train would move on eventually.' Luckily Miranda and I were in a dark corner and escaped unseen.

There was a spontaneously happy meeting with the entire Marañon family, eight altogether counting husband and wife and two children.

Don Gregorio was powerfully built with a head suggestive of a noble Roman. He had large brown eyes which turned easily from gay to grave. His wife was petite, alert, quick in gesture and repartee, and *chata*, which roughly means that she had a small snub nose, a characteristic envied by Spanish women and greatly appreciated by Spanish men – among others. Only one member of the family came properly into focus that afternoon: the youngest daughter, Mabél – who still reminds me of her mother in many ways. There was more talking than listening, quite usual in Spanish gatherings, but suddenly I heard a near-perfect English intonation at my elbow. It turned out that Mabél, for she was speaking, had in her childhood had a governess called Miss Burns of all names.

When it was time for me to leave she told me that she would be away until Christmas staying on Belmonte's ranch in Andalusia. I was surprised to find myself quite downcast by this news after such a brief encounter. Then things took an unexpected turn. By chance we met again a week later at a cocktail party of 'all Madrid', in the current phrase. It seemed natural that we should gravitate towards each other across the crowded room and that it would seem empty apart from her presence. She left for Belmonte's the next day. Then, after a few weeks came an invitation from Belmonte himself, to visit him for a few days with Sebastian Miranda. My big Vauxhall was under repair. I borrowed an old Ford, quite unsuitable for the journey, and set off without more ado.

The *finca* was typical of that region: white, low-built with thick walls, tiled floors with rugs. There were great log fires at that time of year. It overlooked a small bullring where young cows would be tested for breeding, and acres of grassland spotted with Spanish oak: the *ganadería* – fighting bulls, cows and calves – grazed peacefully in the distance. Belmonte was the ideal host: unobtrusive, giving warmth of ease and good company. Miranda had an inexhaustible flow of picaresque anecdote, well matched by Belmonte. This left Mabél and myself relaxed spectators, tired from hard riding and long walks. We were given the chance of being on our own without the pressure of time or anyone's curiosity. It was there and thereafter that we dropped the use of our Christian names and have addressed each other with the Spanish *tu* ever since. 'So many people call you Tom,' Mabél explained enigmatically, but I saw the point. After a few days it was time for me to return to Madrid. I sensed that a new dimension was beginning to take form for both of us.

With Miranda as passenger, there was again a bizarre happening. My little car had no heater and it was bitterly cold on that endless road across La Mancha. Suddenly, as we passed through a village, we narrowly missed a flock of turkeys being driven by a woman with a long stick. 'Stop!' said Miranda. He dismounted, haggled with the woman and came back with two enormous birds under his arms. 'They'll keep us warm,' and indeed they did, settling peacefully between our legs, occasionally rearing an inquisitive head, giving us fits of laughter on the cheerless road. The birds were well rewarded, being sumptuously fattened for the Christmas feast.

Just after Christmas Mabél and I stole a day for ourselves away from Madrid, driving to Alcala de Henares, an ancient university town nearby. Not much was said in the old scholars' refectory turned restaurant, nor in the awesome *aula* or lecture-hall. At the end of the day, in a tumbledown *taberna* on the outskirts of Madrid, we rested before separating for that night. It was there that what we must have been groping towards in the past few weeks came clearly into sight. Now we were looking not so much at each other as in the same direction. We were going to be married: to enter a different condition of humanity where it can be co-creative of the race and the origin of a new causality. We did not think, of course, in those philosophical terms but that does not invalidate the reality, which only the Church remembers and recalls without ceasing. It was a singularly unpropitious place for such a tremendous mutation to take place, crammed with noisy customers, open to the dusty road, but to me the bread and the wine had a sacramental quality.

I did not lose much time in looking for the symbolic engagement gift. In Spain, instead of a ring, the *novia* is usually presented with a bracelet. My gift was of little gold bricks strung together in four rows: each brick convenient for a separate inscription on the reverse. To encapsulate, this is the sequence of the first eight inscriptions: *Toledo* (10.10.43) – that was our first meeting; *Quintanar* (17.10.43) – the Marqueses of that name were hosts of the party already mentioned; *Juan* (4.12.43) – this was when the visit to the *finca* began; *Alcala* (28.12.43) – has just been explained; *Sam* (1.1.44) was when I sought the ambassador's official permission to marry; *Cypher* (3.2.44) was when the Foreign Office telegram of agreement arrived; *Peticion* (18.4.44.) was the date of a dinner party at the embassy when the formal 'asking the hand' took place; and the simple date 29.4.44 marks the wedding at the Royal Church of San Jeronimo. At that time there were many bricks awaiting inscription. The bracelet is full now with the names of four children (and our first who died at birth), with their marriages and their children and some milestones in our life together. There is no room for anything else.

Our wedding was something of a public event and became known as the *Boda de Gasolina* because, quite accidentally, it coincided with the Allies' lifting of the embargo on petrol imports. It was given the full treatment in the official newsreels in the cinema. Showing, as it did, Anglo-Spanish friendship in a wide social spectrum, it marked a popular, as distinct from an official, welcome to the British presence and mission in Spain. We were no longer there under sufferance.

None of this welcome could have happened, of course,

without the Marañon *mystique*, not to speak of the Marañon family's arrangements for the whole affair. It was at once solemn and popular. The Marañon family chaplain, a wizened little priest of great age, was to perform the marriage ceremony. Mgr Henson, the bluff bulldog rector of the English College in Valladolid, was to say the nuptial Mass. The chaplain had been enjoined (and had agreed) to keep his homily very short. In the event it went on and on, recalling everything from my bride's childhood onwards. I could see Mgr Henson, vested for Mass, waiting at the door to the sanctuary, champing like a bull in the *toril* waiting to rush into the ring. We were married, according to an old Spanish custom, *bajo vela*, whereby a large lace cloth is draped over the bride's head and the bridegroom's shoulders: one cloth covering what was now to be one flesh.

The church had a cloister admirably suited to jollification on a large scale. In the end we drove off to the Marañon country place for a few days of solitude and peace. Then we started on a trip south which included luncheon with the Governor of Gibraltar – but with hardly a memory of my previous visit. When we reached Granada there was a message to say that Arthur Yencken had been killed in an air crash on the way to Barcelona. This meant an all-night drive back to Madrid to be present at the funeral. It was a solemn affair; according to custom the head of a mission who dies *en poste* is given all the funeral honours of a general fallen in battle; the Spaniards rose to the occasion and I followed the cortège on foot along the main avenue.

I was walking back into the pressures and problems that beset the embassy each day. I would plead for a loosening-up of the continued hostility of the press and the totalitarian impositions of the regime. There was now a glimmer of change. Franco occasionally would make drastic changes in the government without warning to the public or the persons concerned.

General Jordana, who had replaced Suñer as foreign minister, died and had to be hurriedly replaced. Franco's choice of a successor was of a very different kidney: José-Felix de Lequerica, a *simpático* and cynical Basque. He had been Spain's ambassador in Paris for most of the German occupation, and a good friend of the Marañons, in exile there. So it happened that he was one of the first dinner guests in our home, we being newly married. We agreed to settle for the English custom, for once, of separating the sexes at the end of dinner to give the minister a chance to expand and let his indiscretions roll. He did so, far into the night to the despair of the ladies. I got a good glimpse into the rapidly changing positions of Spanish diplomacy. Fresh from his contacts with the German High Command in Paris, Laquerica was scenting the possibility of the defeat of Nazism.

But de Lequerica's term of office was short-lived and Franco's totally surprise choice of a successor was my friend Alberto Martin Artajo. I happened to be with him when the news broke. I could not help asking him bluntly how he could accept the appointment given his liberal views. 'I will always have the option of resignation, if I need it,' he answered without taking offence. He seemed unaware of the fact that General Franco did not accept resignations any more than refusals to take office. His ministers were regarded as sentries who stood at their posts until they were replaced.

But, of course, the whole political atmosphere had changed and Martin Artajo got the job because he was a good lawyer used to dealing with the irreconcilable and settling complicated questions of inheritance, responsibility and the like. General Franco had many delicate adjustments to make and a need for new understandings: Martin Artajo was his man and became increasingly so as I watched him ever more deeply embedded in the regime. They called him 'the pious elephant' in his own ministry (he was a devout Catholic and heavily built). His relations with the British ambassador were cordial, but both men seemed to prefer to leave some grey areas for informal talk between him and myself. A first secretary could not officially call on a foreign minister so his car would be sent to pick me up and waft us off to the country. On one such occasion he took me up near to the Escorial where 'the Valley of the Fallen' was being excavated from a mountainside of solid rock by Republican prisoners of war (some five years after the Nationalist victory!).

'It is to be the greatest monument for all those who died for Spain in our war,' said the minister. It was certainly impressive: a vast tunnel with transepts was being transformed into an underground cathedral with the deafening noise of drills and explosive charges, the rumble of loaded tractors and clouds of stone dust. As we drove away it occurred to me to say that it should be a monument to all who died for Spain irrespective of which side they had fought for. The minister seemed to be horrified and indignant at first, but after a long pause turned to me and said that he agreed. Later I had a letter from him saying that my idea had been put 'to the highest authority in the country' and had been accepted. The fact that 'the Valley of the Fallen' is now *de facto* a monument to Republicans as well as Nationalists is not widely known. In any case, the very idea would be repudiated by all liberal and Republican sympathisers and most right wingers. To visit the place, now that it is completed, is inevitably to be awestruck by the grandiose character, the implacable marble and bronze furnishings of the vast mausoleum where at last Franco and Primo de Rivera, the founder of Falange, are laid to rest.

Martin Artajo was, of course, no Falangist although he had to dress the part. He would urge me to realise what appalling damage had been inflicted on the Spanish people by the Civil War. Its broken limbs must still be kept in Plaster of Paris, was his simile. He urged patience and certainly exemplified it in his own dealings with internal political tensions and the conflicting claims of the belligerent countries.

He was to remain foreign minister until long after the Second World War and to achieve much for the diplomatic rehabilitation of his country. His last act of friendship was to offer my wife and myself a farewell luncheon at the ministry just before our return to London. It was a splendid affair and a far cry from those somewhat furtive and anxious meetings four years earlier when nothing of this kind could have been remotely envisaged; it was also a rare if not unique honour for an out-going first secretary.

The slight easing of the political climate was not reflected in the everyday attempts by all sides to confuse the others. Thanks, I think, to one of our own officers of misinformation, the Germans became convinced that there would be a British landing in Spain. This had the desired effect of upsetting their troop dispositions. There were sharp and anxious enquiries by the Spaniards but we could not very well say that we had invented the whole story.

This reminds me of the famous 'man that never was': the corpse of a British officer washed up on the beach near Huelva in the spring of 1943. Predictably at that time, German Intelligence was alerted first by the Spanish police. The corpse carried papers of apparently supreme importance giving plans for an Allied landing in Sardinia and Greece whereas the actual landing took place in Sicily. The Germans faithfully copied and replaced the papers. The British were next informed and the corpse was given a military burial in Huelva. My 'need to know' about the fictitious 'Major Martin' was confined to 'knowing' about his intelligence, charm and knowledge of Spain through a connection with our Burgos agency in the Civil War. I took all this in good faith, blaming my memory for recalling nothing of it. The ruse was supremely successful and resulted in a large-scale diversion of German troops away from the actual scene of action. But it could easily have been a total failure. After the war I became friendly with the doctor in Huelva who had performed the autopsy. He told me that he was sure that the man had not died from drowning – as had been made to appear – but that he had seen no reason to tell the Germans about this. His silence completed the great deception.

In the last months of the war in Europe my job had virtually come to an end. Some memories recur. I was one of first from the embassy to cross into France after the Armistice to meet a Free-French group which has been engaged in clandestine intelligence and propaganda. I was stopped on the road by a group of armed *maquisards* with armbands. One of them broke into English with the unmistakeable burr of Oxfordshire. Having been cut off from home by the German advance, he had been with the *maquis* throughout the war. He gave me his father's name and address and begged me to make immediate telegraphic contact. That was no problem. Later, a local doctor and resistance leader brought me to his home for lunch. We went to the bottom of his garden and dug out a large glass jar wherein a duck was preserved in aspic. Those were days of great joy.

With VE day in sight the ambassador had made arrangements for his immediate recall. He went with scant ceremony and what I thought was a tasteless expression of delight at leaving Spain, his few Spanish friends and the embassy staff.

To my relief his place was temporarily taken by Jim Bowker as *chargé d'Affaires*. He had been the Head of Chancery in my first year or so and a great standby; his nonchalant charm, impeccable manners and dress concealed great sagacity and a sharp intelligence. With my work virtually over, I was grateful when he offered me extended local leave to settle my personal affairs before leaving at the end of the year. As he said, I had scarcely had a break in five years.

There had been very short visits to London; the first to cope with what I had left hanging in the air when I first went to Madrid, expecting to be there for only a couple of weeks. I had to dispose of my flat and store my possessions (they were moved to a warehouse which was totally burnt out in the Blitz). The second had been with the ambassador for a series of conferences at the Foreign Office. The third was spent in more colourful company: with various Intelligence officers and the SOE where Colonel Gubbins reigned. He took me to dinner with Guy Burgess whom I disliked on sight. 'Set Europe ablaze!' had been Churchill's call to SOE. I scented contingency plans to apply this injunction to Spain if necessary and argued against it forcibly, knowing more than they did of the desert that it would create. On this trip, in the height of the Blitz, small private parties relieved the tension. At one of these, I found Noel Coward; my hostess persuaded him to go to the piano and sing 'London Pride', his own composition and the theme song of the time. It brought back a violent nostalgia for my beloved and now suffering city. This was made the more poignant by the too-brief meetings with a handful of friends. Memories stayed with me as on my departure I found myself bobbing about in a dinghy in Southampton Water, waiting to be ferried to a giant flying boat due to take off as soon as the all-clear sounded from Southampton. By a long circuitous route we eventually came down on the Tagus twinkling with the lights of Lisbon.

On VE day I was given a job which I had never dreamed of: to take over the German Embassy in Madrid. Polite officials from the Spanish Ministry for Foreign Affairs took me along. The Nazis had left nothing behind except for a few office desks. In a drawer in one of them I found a brand new pistol and a few iron crosses which I pocketed. I then went on the roof and hoisted the Union Jack on a tall mast. The memory came back of that row with the young Nazi which I had had in Burgos in the Civil War; and my promise (so rash at the time) that if his country were to crush Czechoslovakia – which then seemed imminent – his regime would be crushed in its turn.

A quite unexpected letter from Douglas Jerrold of the publishers Eyre & Spottiswoode arrived from London inviting me to take charge of Burns & Oates on my return. It fulfilled an ambition that I had harboured almost since boyhood. Oblique suggestions from the SIS that I might wish for some permanent employment with them could now be discouraged with safety for the future. Samuel Hoare was good enough to write in his memoirs that under my 'vigorous direction, an insignificant section of the Embassy had developed into a great and imposing organisation'. I felt that I could leave it at that.

One day Brigadier Torr, the miliary attaché, burst into my room. 'Congratulations, Tom, you are a "Call-me-God" in the embassy's honours list.' I had not expected a CMG – and perhaps just as well as in fact I never received it. Back in London I was asked to lunch by the then head of the Ministry of Information, Sir Kenneth Grubb. I knew him slightly from the early days of war when he was in charge of the Latin American section of the ministry. His Latin American experience was confined to many years spent on that continent as an evangelical lay missionary. Certainly he had the zeal that would be required for the job and a hatred of 'Rome' which seemed to go with it. What other qualifications he possessed are conjectural. My contact with the Ministry of Information had been restricted to routine matters, my real work lying elsewhere. At the coffee stage of our lunch my host suddenly remarked with a characteristic smirk that served as a smile: 'By the way, I'm sorry that I had to knock you off the embassy honours list; I thought too many RCs were getting gongs.'

With Mabél I was in San Sebastian with the rest of the embassy staff in the summer of 1945 and our baby was due to be born in October. He appeared a month before his time but there was virtually no apparatus for premature births in the nursing home which was used in this emergency. He survived just two days. I can still remember giving him the kiss of life to no avail. With his little white coffin on my knees I was alone in the car which took us to the cemetery where I laid him in the vault of close relations of my wife's family. A brief candle had flickered and gone out, leaving us a darkness all our own. But the faith and courage of *el Inglesito*'s mother overcame that darkness in the end. I had not seen the like in all my life.

There came a time to say goodbye. The Chancery had seen staff changes over the years but the principal attachés had been with me all along. Chief among these was the naval attaché, Captain Alan Hillgarth, the *eminence grise* of the place. He had quarter-deck manners and a conspiratorial style of talking out of the side of his mouth. He was a personal friend of Churchill's, more so than was the ambassador, and this direct line had been invaluable at critical times. Without any proselytism on my part he greatly surprised me one day by asking me to be his godfather for reception into the Catholic Church. Later this also happened with Christopher Bramwell, who had come to the embassy as Head of Chancery. Faith is something caught rather than taught and I can only put their conversions down to something infectious in the Spanish air, because I had never discussed religion with my two new godsons. I was in close touch with both of them after the war, until they died, before their time. I served Christopher's Requiem at the Brompton Oratory.

Alan Lubbock, the assistant military attaché, had been a gunner in the Great War. He was a Hampshire squire and, after a second war, Lord Lieutenant of the county. He was a Wykehamist with a passion for the classics as well as the finer points of sherry. He was robust and fastidious and shared with me the delights of the smells, noise and exotic *platos* of the little *tabernas* ensconced in the old quarter of Madrid.

In total contrast was Hugh Ellis-Rees of the Treasury, of immense affability and superbly efficient in his job. He headed the Economic section with the over-elegant David Eccles, later a Cabinet minister. They were a formidable pair. I introduced them to sucking pig and rough wine on their arrival. David was no stranger to Spain but Hugh – with little Spanish – soon made his mark on the Spanish Ministry of Industry and Commerce. These two created the solid sub-structure for the hard bargaining that went on with the ministry. Spain depended on our navi-certs allowing vital imports, so that this ministry was largely free from the hostile ideology of Falangism. Hugh, otherwise the most insular man imaginable, was a devout Catholic; he lost his heart to Spain; later he became chairman of the Anglo-Spanish society in London, having been ambassador to the OECD in Paris.

There was a great team spirit in the place with many other friends too numerous to mention, but these men, and above all Arthur Yencken, were of my special confidence.

Spanish friends were legion. Part of my job had been to be on familiar terms with *madrileños* of every kind. The Chancery moved in its traditional groove, largely insulated from ordinary people. But I brought the Spaniards in droves to my film shows, to get contacts. For me, it had all started with that lonely prophetic lunch which had ended up with joining the famous *tertulia*. I moved around everywhere from the Ritz to the *rastro* (flea market), deliberately making myself recognisable and available. I had made myself 'the most observed of all observers' and this – like charity – covered a multitude of other operations which were necessarily more discreet.

For the Spaniards I devised a farewell Christmas card – an engraving of St Paul's Cathedral together with Dr Johnson's conclusion that 'the man who is tired of London is tired of life'. It was a hint that I was returning to where my true loyalty had rested through all the intrigues and enchantments of Madrid. During that parenthetical appointment, nothing was quite what it seemed to be and nobody was quite himself.

10

Of Coteries and Clubs

The war had mixed everyone together, at least in the milieu that was mine. Catholics were almost indistinguishable from their fellow countrymen. The analogy of a blended whisky supplanting a pure malt is not wide of the mark.

In the later 1920s there still existed a discernible phenomenon, what Bloomsbury would call a Catholic sub-culture, what I regarded as a super-culture. Today it occupies high places in the Establishment but then it was an alternative community inhabiting a fortress rather than a ghetto. Hereditary Catholics were joined then by the new intellectual converts and lived very happily apart from the rest. I was not of ancient Catholic lineage nor was I a convert but my publishing activities brought me into their gatherings.

In some ways the old-established Wiseman Society was a typical one. It held its periodical dinners at Claridge's – white tie was *de rigueur*. Dowagers brought their daughters in the hope of meeting 'suitable' young men. Elderly men of letters (an Alfred Noyes, an Algernon Cecil) mingled with retired diplomats and obscure peers.

I suppose that Billy Clonmore (later the Earl of Wicklow) and I were among the youngest members of the Wiseman. One of the dinners is especially memorable. G. K. Chesterton was the speaker. I was seated at a long oval table, Billy was at the other end. The other occupants were elderly and sedate. Came the Loyal Toast and permission to smoke. A dreary peer was introducing G. K. at inordinate length. Billy had lit a long cigar and was nodding over his coffee and, as it happened, over a match-standard. At one nod, deeper than the rest, the cigar touched the match-standard which went up like a Roman candle. Billy's characteristic fuzzy forelock was singed but, now wide awake, he kept his head. He reached for a menu card and scribbled my name and a message, 'Please pass it on.' His neighbour happened to be the saintly Superior of Farm Street. I noticed raised eyebrows as the menu was passed on to me. Billy had written on it a simple expletive of four letters. It was his last appearance at the dinners.

After the Second World War the Wiseman was reincarnated, in black tie and less exalted surroundings. I was elected chairman but after just one dinner I realised that the society was totally effete and I persuaded the Committee to dissolve it.

In many ways Chris Hollis typified the new blend. He was the son of an Anglican bishop, a colleger at Eton and a member of Pop, winner of the Brackenbury prize at Oxford where he became a Catholic under the influence, in human terms, of the Chester-Belloc and of Douglas Woodruff. He was an incessant talker with the maddening Etonian habit of interrupting one in the course of argument. His frequent bursts of laughter sounded like the neighing of a horse. His manners were not bad, they were non-existent.

But he had many endearing qualities of which moral courage and humility were foremost. I published his first book, a slim volume on Glastonbury ('Here was England born and made and murdered,' he wrote) in 1927 and he produced a succession of popular biographies from St Ignatius to Lenin, as well as a book, *The American Heresy* (1929), which caught the eye of President Roosevelt and his New Dealers, who recruited him for a time. He taught history to the sixth form at Stonyhurst for many years before the war and became deeply attached to the spirit of the place which even by then retained a recusant flavour.

If the Christopher Hollis ingredient contributed his convert spirit to the blended whisky in my analogy, so did Christopher Sykes, a traditional Catholic, the pure malt. From a Yorkshire family, he went to the Sorbonne for a year and so on to Christ

Church, Oxford, with perfect French. After a spell in minor diplomatic posts at Berlin and Teheran he turned to journalism and travelled widely in Persia and Afghanistan.

When we first met, in 1935, Christopher was beginning a life of authorship and I published his first book, *Wassmus* (1936), the life of a romantic German figure (similar in some way to Lawrence of Arabia) who tried to raise Persian nationalists against the British in the First World War. In a way this was a prophesy of his own war which ranged from intelligence duties in Cairo to service with the SAS in Occupied France. After the war writing worked on him like a drug. He would read, with a most endearing stutter, bits of his writing to me with relish.

That arch-reactionary Monsignor Talbot opined that it was the proper duty of Catholic laymen 'to hunt, to shoot and to entertain'. Christopher did all three but his interest in the varieties of religious experience never palled and his Benedictine education assured a love of the liturgy. He could not bear the innovations of Vatican II. His zest for life and wide human sympathies made him an excellent biographer. With one foot in his old Catholic camp and another in White's he typified a transitional period as the upper levels of the Catholic community merged with its surroundings. Following a long illness in 1978 he chose to go, against all medical advice, to the family home of Sledmen. After an exorbitant dinner to celebrate his home-coming, he went to bed and died in his sleep.

A London club is, like the poet's grave, 'a fine and private place / but none I think do there embrace,' nor do they talk about it outside, except for a few moles (possibly guests) who occasionally throw crumbs to the gossip writers. The Garrick is discretion itself in this matter, but a word about the Old Burgundians is not out of turn.

It started as a joke, after the war. Daniel Macmillan (who

seemed to have scant respect for his younger brother, the Prime Minister) used to preside daily at a corner table which about a dozen of convivial members monopolised: Bill Casey, then editor of *The Times*; Patrick Ryan, a leader writer on the paper; Stanley Morison; Frank Lawton, an actor; Orlo Williams, a gentle and musical civil servant and a lover of Dante; Douglas Jerrold, Osbert Lancaster, Robert Lutyens, Arthur Ransome, Felix Aylmer and T. S. Eliot.

Good wine was in short supply even at the Garrick in the post-war period. Dan, one day in May 1950, suggested that a club be formed to dine monthly with better vintages. We called it 'The Old Burgundians'. It mainly consisted of the *habitués* of the table. The secretaryship fell to me with the tricky responsibility for choosing the wine and the food. Robin Darwin, another member, was the head of the Royal College of Art and undertook to have a special tie designed for us. It was a splendid object with broad bands of Claret and Burgundy colours and a thinner line of champagne colour between them. Nobody dared to dine without his tie (even Morison would forsake his habitual black one for the occasion). We enjoyed ourselves for many years, but the club gradually shrunk as its members died one by one, temporarily flickering into new vigour with the transfusion of new blood in the persons of Gerry Noël, Kenneth More, Robert Speaight and others. To one of its meetings I came straight from Dan's flat in Grosvenor Square where his life was slipping away. I suggested to my ribald companions a minute of silent prayer. The Catholics (who were in a majority) welcomed the idea, others were embarrassed as if I had suggested a sexual orgy. The club died in 1967, three years after the death of its founder and, indeed, of all its original members except myself.

Though his active membership of the Old Burgundians was brief Tom Eliot enjoyed the convivial club-within-a-club atmosphere. When I come to think of him – as indeed I do quite often – it is in episodes. I came to *The Wasteland* too early: its sophistication had no echo in my immature experience. But *Ash Wednesday* was another matter. Love of a poem, as of a person, comes before understanding, distant calls and hints in my mind challenged a pursuit. Years earlier, one of my sisters asked me for an exegesis. I did a good deal of research into its sources in other poetry and mythology. I was surprised by the result and, greatly daring, sent it to the poet in homage. To my surprise and joy came a letter saying I had put more into the poem than he himself thought it carried. He invited me to tea in his Faber & Faber office. 'The aged eagle', as I called him to my friends, was kindness itself. He suggested that I might like to come to a luncheon club of his.

Of course I accepted and we went to a pub near the Victoria and Albert Museum. I cannot remember its name but it had a covered patio and wicker chairs, a sort of winter garden. The *venue* had been chosen for the convenience of Arthur Wheen, an ascetic Australian, a member of the museum staff, an ex-infantry man of David Jones vintage and experience (they later became friends). Other members that I remember were Richard Church, a subtle novelist and civil servant; Bonamy Dobree, more like a bluff major than a professor of literature, though he was both; Herbert Read who I used to call 'the gentle anarchist' who was to become a friend (eventually I wrote an introduction to his *Form in Modern Poetry* which I published in my *Essays in Order*) and Alec Randall, a devout Catholic, a diplomat and a specialist in modern German and French literature. Much later he was to be of the greatest help in my tenure of *The Tablet* editorship.

These men were the mainstay of *The Criterion*, Eliot's quarterly, which was a sort of lighthouse shedding its beam over the rocks and cross-currents and fog which characterised the intellectual world at that time.

I never wanted to bother a genius with the over-load of work and personal worry which Eliot bore so patiently. But a sparrow is of the same species as an eagle and we had much mutual understanding. 'Tom,' I said once, 'I wish you weren't a heretic.' 'I'm not, I'm a schismatic,' he answered quietly without taking any offence as, of course, none was intended. Much later, reading Newman, I noted that when he came precisely to that realisation he went over to Rome without hesitation.

After the war, and up to when he began his very happily married life, Tom Eliot and I met often at the Garrick at a long table in the corner where talk was casual and free. Here Eliot was in his most relaxed mood. He was lunching there on the day that his Nobel Prize was announced. I congratulated him (it had not occurred to anyone else at the table to do so).

'Well, at last I'll be able to do up my bathroom,' he said.

Due to increasing ill-health, he withdrew from club life. For me he still lives and speaks in his poetry as one more evangelist.

Back to Publishing

Burns & Oates had seen many changes in its over 100-year history. It began in 1836 as plain James Burns, bookseller and publisher, a respectable High Anglican firm in Portman Square. It ceased to exist as such when, as I have already mentioned, its then owner, my great uncle James Burns, followed his friend Newman into the Catholic Church. In 1847, Newman helped to rebuild the business as a Catholic publishing house, Burns & Oates, with the gift of his novel *Loss and Gain*, of *Assent* and other works. A golden period was that of Wilfred Meynell who joined the firm about 1900 and left active management in 1919. The firm became a by-word for typography under the influence of his son, Francis Meynell and Stanley Morison.

It diversified in 1921 by taking on R & T Washbourne, specialists in *bondieuserie* of all kinds. In 1929 it was taken over by the Hutchinson group of publishers which put in two retired colonels to manage it, good men who knew nothing of the trade. Rescue from an inevitable decline in its fortunes came in 1939 from Eyre & Spottiswoode, the Crown Printers, who also owned a publishing firm of the same name.

The chairman of the whole concern when I came back to London was Oliver Crosthwaite-Eyre, a mercurial young Tory MP straight from service in the Marines. His managing director was Douglas Jerrold whom I had known by chance before the war and was by now an old friend. Neither had much enthusiasm for religious publishing as such but I am sure that Oliver had bought Burns & Oates from Hutchinson for religious reasons rather than for profit.

The whole scene was rather more complex than I had expected. The pious objects division was incongruously under the management of a former captain of the Gurkhas, a hard-bitten character with little taste for his new trade. Then the fertile brain of Douglas Jerrold had invented another imprint for secular books to be a subsidiary of Burns & Oates. He called it Hollis & Carter for no other reason than the chance of having Chris Hollis – by now a popular Catholic writer and MP – for a nominal chairman. Carter, a former inspector of schools, was recruited to attract some educational books. But I never saw Mr Carter at any board meeting and there were no educational books in the list. Another director was the all-round sportsman C. B. Fry – an idol of my youth – very elegant with a monocle and an endless stream of chat on every conceivable subject except matters that happened to be up for discussion. Finally, there was a genial old crony of Jerrold's from the Authors' Club, Ernest Short, who was brimful of enthusiasm and foisted on us two scissors-and-paste art books which were published – at a foreseeable loss – out of deference to his years and to make up for an exiguous salary.

Hollis & Carter might well have become a viable business on its own. Friends rallied round when I took it in hand and I soon had the beginnings of a civilised list. Larry Kirwan, the secretary of the Royal Geographical Society, produced a definitive history of Polar exploration; Michael Richey, by now secretary of the Royal Institute of Navigation, edited a masterly treatise on the haven-finding art. Roy Campbell's *Light on a Dark Horse* (1951) was a hilarious autobiography. In those days, and because all concerned were still living, I had to bowdlerise his vivid account of Harold Nicholson's homosexual advances towards him and Vita Sackville-West's reciprocated lesbian passion for his wife Mary. 'But it's all true, Tom,' exploded Roy, 'they can't go to court because they *know* it.' Nevertheless I judged, with Newman, in another context, that 'certain truths are inexpedient'.

That fine Spanish liberal scholar, Salvador de Madariaga, gave me his two-volume work on the rise and fall of the Spanish

American empire which effectively destroyed the 'black legend' about the *conquistadores*.

Belloc's literary executors appointed Robert Speaight as the authorised biographer. This enraged Belloc's daughter and son-in-law who wanted J. B. Morton, a life-long friend, to do the job. From a vast mass of material they gave Speaight just one postcard of Belloc's when he turned up at Belloc's old home with an empty suitcase to collect the treasure that he reasonably expected. The gap was filled to some extent by the publication of the *Letters of Hilaire Belloc* which he edited later.

The C. B. Fry connection, as well as Christopher Hollis's devotion to the game, produced a plethora of books about cricket. The autobiography of Jack Hobbs was the most successful of them all. We launched it in the members' room at the Oval. I can still see that wizened witty king of batsmen gazing out over the rain-soaked ground – the scene of so many of his triumphs. My interest in all things Spanish led me to publish a seminal book by Menendez Pidal, *The Spaniards in their history*; also three biographies by my father-in-law Gregorio Marañon.

Publishers in those days were shy of books critical of the Soviet Union. I was delighted to take on Trotsky's life of Stalin. I had a visit from some wimpish character at the Foreign Office who had got wind of the book and tried to show me how inopportune its publication would be.

I published Anthony Nutting whom I had known at the embassy in Madrid. He became Minister of State at the Foreign Office but resigned this post and his seat in Parliament as a protest against Anthony Eden's Suez policy. He revealed the whole sordid background to the Suez plot in *I Saw for Myself* (1958), after the crisis.

★   ★   ★

Such were the main lines of the Hollis & Carter list – as good as any – but it failed to pay its way from the point of view of the holdings board. I see now that its Burns & Oates association was a drawback. It needed quite separate marketing, without any hint of its parental influence. I sold it to the Bodley Head, which in its turn is now part of a vast impersonal conglomerate.

My principle *raison d'être*, to revive a moribund Catholic list, was going to be a long haul as the old firm, Burns & Oates, for all its world-wide reputation, had only survived on its fine series of liturgical works. There was simply no reflection of contemporary Catholic thought in its list.

But I had three advantages. First, paper rationing had been a great equaliser in the publishing world; competition was not fierce and virtually every book published at this time sold out, such was the scarcity of reading matter. Secondly, export markets were opening up after many years. And, thirdly, new Catholic talent was emerging after the barren years of the war.

There was confusion, uncertainty and risk in this evolving situation but it held out some promise. I was not in ultimate control of the situation until, after two years, Crosthwaite-Eyre came along with an offer to sell the business to me and my associates. It was an awesome offer but the terms were not too onerous. I accepted and began some restructuring which was not completed until BOW Holdings was created which came to own the publishing firm, its retail shops, *The Tablet* and finally the *Universe*, a popular weekly which I abhorred but which was highly profitable.

My Gurkha captain – to his delight – was moved to Australia to run our new agency there; my eccentric Hollis & Carter board had been disbanded long since and I became chairman of the holding company as well as the two publishing imprints. This situation held for twenty years.

I was greatly helped at an early stage by the advent of David James. He was an ex-RNVR officer, highly decorated for his gallantry as a remarkable escaper from a prisoner-of-war camp. He was an Etonian with that touch of assurance and omni-competence which that school seems to create in its better products. He was an ardent convert, having been received into the Church in the prison camp. He was well off and offered substantial investment in the company. We became firm friends but before long he was elected to Parliament and our interests inevitably tended to diverge. He died before his time.

I had to begin with a skeleton staff but gradually formed a team. In due course I had three young and very able assistants: Simon King as editor, Anthony Clarke as sales manager, and my nephew Paul Burns in charge of production. I could not have had a better or happier band. We worked together in an informal atmosphere, without regard to hours or effort.

After a couple of years things were going badly for us in Australia. The Gurkha captain had apparently not endeared himself to the locals and Australian booksellers were making it clear that they didn't want a 'pommy' involved in their affairs. It was decided that I should go out and settle matters according to my judgement on the spot.

An unexpected bonus of the trip was the chance to visit other Burns & Oates agents on the way. At Singapore, my first stop, we had an agent called Mr Chong. I called at his warehouse. An impassive Chinaman was squatting on his doorstep smoking a pipe.

'May I see Mr Chong?'

'I am Mr Chong.'

He was a friendly soul; we inspected stock and I showed him copies of new books. It was a modest trade but I was impressed to see the firm so well known in this distant corner of the globe. Mr Chong invited me to lunch at a vast open-air restaurant and some twenty relatives and friends sat down at a big round table. Slowly dealing with an interminable series of dishes, helped by hot towels in that sweltering place, I suddenly noticed the odd behaviour of a guest immediately opposite. 'Is there something wrong with your cousin?' I asked.

'No worry. He drunk.'

The meal went on without incident.

I thought fit to call on the local bishop – a Frenchman from the Basque country. A bearded man in dungarees was weeding the front garden of his modest palace.

'Is the bishop at home?'

'I am the bishop.'

The Basques are among my favourite people and we shared a bottle of good wine in his sparsely furnished home. All this – as on so many other occasions – gave me a strong sense of the universal brotherhood of the Church. It was the same with the bishop of Darwin, my first stop in Australia. He met me at the airport in shirtsleeves on a sweltering evening and put me up for the night. We consumed large quantities of lager; he was a true brother in Christ.

Another brother was the night porter at the Melbourne Club, where I was able to stay thanks to my membership of the Garrick. One night, as I came in late, he said: 'Excuse me, sir, I hope you don't mind me asking, but *are you one of us?*' (Pause for my comprehension of the question.)

'Well, as a matter of fact I am. What made you think so?'

'Well, sir, you get up early on a Sunday and take *The Advocate* [a Catholic paper]. There are not many of us in this club ... I remember a gentleman, a member for many years, who I thought was one of us. One night he comes in late, rather merry-like, and I says *Dominus vobiscum*. He says *Et cum spiritu tuo* – so I *knew* he was one of us.'

'We', in the porter's sense, were very numerous in Melbourne although the club was strictly of the Protestant ascendancy. Archbishop Mannix, over ninety, very tall and thin with fine white hair, ruled his flock as would an Irish parish priest, with affectionate dictatorship. He was a walking beacon in the city and his telephone number (like himself) was Melbourne 1.

Mannix had been a wanted man when his edict, 'Killing is no murder,' went forth in Ireland against the Black and Tans, and the Vatican had moved him across the world. Now he was as gentle and courteous as could be and very helpful in my business problems. I went on to Sydney and Adelaide and the fascination of Australia with its spontaneity and brash friendliness grew on me. I left the Gurkha captain happy with a modest pension.

My images of India on the homeward flight are still bright.

Madras had a little Catholic colony which welcomed me. I was taken to the reputed shrine of St Thomas the Apostle; a humble place, scarcely visited, but I became convinced of the presence of this headstrong man, who had recovered his lost belief in Jesus from the evidence of his senses, and against his will.

Then there came Calcutta with its avenues of human dereliction: approaching the city centre from the airport, the road is lined for mile after mile with the dung-coloured, dung-constructed hovels of the furtive inhabitants, barely existing in the squalor. Their Hindu religion teaches them reincarnation in better or worse circumstances, so they exist with a faint glimmer of hope, or of resignation. In the city itself their sacred cows blunder about, squatting on the tramlines, shitting in the shops, gaunt pot-bellied creatures that seemed the very incarnation of existence without purpose. It is indeed a wonder that graceful figures in spotless white also go about the ordinary tasks in that modern city and that these are performed efficiently in an atmosphere of chaos.

For me a valuable visit was to the great Jesuit University of St Francis Xavier. The students are virtually all Hindus and no attempt is made at their conversion. I saw the portrait of Rabindranath Tagore in the gallery of distinguished old *alumni*. I was delighted to find among the Hindu specialists, long-bearded Spaniards and young French Jesuits who virtually adopt the Hindu way of life: it struck me that they knew more about Hinduism than most of its practitioners.

Bombay was different – with the coexistence of East and West more evident. I had an agent there in the person of Benny Aguiar, the redoubtable editor of *The Bombay Examiner*, a fine open-minded Catholic weekly. He later wrote frequently for me in *The Tablet* and to my astonishment still carries on. Cardinal Gracias, the Primate of All-India, invited me to lunch with his clergy. The cardinal, a Goanese, was an imposing figure, very tall and slim with the most gracious manners. He was the first native bishop of the see; his predecessors were drawn from the English province of the Jesuits. Archbishop Roberts, the last of them, was a prophetic figure and virtually forced Rome to make the change. The cardinal's lunch was a very grand affair, with fragrant curries in abundance, but courtesy over-reached itself in my case; a plate of bacon and eggs being put before me. It seemed to me the *viaticum* of the departed British Raj.

The British Commissioner offered many facilities but would not let me venture in Bombay by night without his tough security officer in a car. Just as the sacred cows in Bombay are all corralled to prevent their deplorable intrusion into normal life as happens in Calcutta, so too are Bombay's prostitutes, pimps, perverts, transvestites and drug-peddlers confined to a big square. Here are the famous cages where listless prostitutes display themselves in the hope of some commercial copulation. The square itself is bedlam and no European who valued his skin will venture there on foot. Here the most wretched specimens of humanity drag out an inhuman existence, awaiting, as I believe, their redemption in the next world.

Back in London problems and opportunities abounded. By chance I recently came across a Burns & Oates catalogue for 1962. There are more than 1,000 books listed and practically all were published in my time. The list ranges from children's books to the magisterial volumes of Copleston's *History of Philosophy*. I reissued a series of spiritual classics in the 'Orchard Series' which ranged from the *Confessions* of St Augustine to the *Autobiography* of St Teresa of Avila. To this I added 'The Golden Library' of shorter books of the same *genre*. In the trade such are called bread-and-butter books. Truly it was a question of casting one's bread on the water to return after many days. They tied up capital but it was well invested; sooner or later they would all be sold.

The 'Faith and Fact' books was a more ambitious project, undertaken with a French and an American publisher: 150 short books covering the whole area of modern knowledge in relation to Catholic teaching. New names were emerging from Europe: German authors such as Rahner, Guardini and Gorres, French such as de Lubac and Thibon, and from the United States Thomas Merton. These were the forerunners of the great renaissance inspired by and inspiring the Vatican Council.

For me, the climax of my publishing effort was the publication of a new international review of theology, *Concilium*, in which Burns & Oates worked in close collaboration with publishers in France, Holland, Germany, Italy and Spain. We met at regular intervals in one country or another together with leading theologians from each country under the inspiration of Hans Küng. Our gatherings were serious seminars, planning issues months ahead, but congenial and convivial events as well. We were almost a little council on our own, not infrequently frowned upon by the Roman authorities. Happily this great enterprise continues, although Burns & Oates had to pass on their edition to the safe hands of Messrs Nelson.

If *Concilium* permitted some excesses in speculation, to my mind these compensated for accretions of superstition in the past life of the Church. Orthodoxy, according to Chesterton, stands reeling but erect between the heresies which individuals engender. We liked to think of ourselves, in the phrase of Cardinal Suenens, as 'at the extreme centre'.

One job to which I gave special care was the definitive edition of the Knox bible on Oxford India paper. From the point of view of production I think it still holds its own among modern bibles. I had the expert help of Stanley Morison for the typography, and the printer of the Cambridge University Press, Brooke Crutchley. The Cambridge University Press composed the type and the Oxford University Press printed it by offset – which gave it a very special parentage. *Pace* Evelyn Waugh's life of Ronald Knox – *Ronald Knox* (1959) – the latter showed a polite interest in the production but none of the enthusiasm with which Waugh credits him. Publication was celebrated by a large luncheon at the Hyde Park Hotel with Cardinal Griffin in the chair and the then Minister of Education, David Eccles, as a guest. Ronnie Knox was showing signs of his malignant illness but kept up a front of wry humour.

The lunch was something of a Belshazzar's feast for me. I saw the writing on the wall for the publishing branch of BOW Holdings. All its profit was earned by *The Universe*, all its losses were incurred by book publishing and by *The Tablet*. I would have been content with the overall profits of the group. The holdings board was not. It consisted of a chartered accountant, a City lawyer, an MP, the editor of *The Universe* and Douglas Woodruff, in poor health. None of them had any interest in my books except as merchandise – never as messages. But I had the moral support of my senior staff and that was what mattered to me.

Eventually, and almost with relief, I agreed to a voluntary liquidation and set about finding the best solution to our troubles. I had been increasingly linked with Herder of Freibourg over various projects and to me the ideal arrangement would be for that great international publisher to take over our list. I knew that they were considering a London branch. We fitted the bill, it seemed to me, and so it did to Herman Herder who came over to see me at my invitation. After a great deal of dogged discussion in London and Freibourg the deal was struck. We sold our entire stock and our contracts and I rejoiced to think that the most solid Catholic publisher in Europe would be carrying on a publishing policy after my own heart.

It is part of the Burns & Oates story – but no longer my story – that after three years of ownership, Herder seemed to lose their nerve. What should have been an exercise in retrenchment turned into a disorderly retreat. Something seems to have cracked in the German psyche and they ignominiously shut down their Burns & Oates branch. Stocks were dispersed and sold in a hugger-mugger way, contracts were left in the air. Doubtless Herder had great problems of their own. The whole world of Catholic publishing went awry with the Vatican Council and the consequent mutation of the Church. Supreme prudence not panic might have weathered the storm. Herder even let our centennial imprint go. I am happy to know that today it is in the careful hands of Search Press, a pioneering publishing house going back to the 1960s, who bought the imprint and recruited my nephew Paul Burns. So the imprint survives with some books of the original list and many additions including pioneer works of liberation theology: it is alive and growing again. I cannot help thinking that the spirit of James Burns, a man of faith, courage and even holiness, has had something to do with the indestructibility of his foundation.

If there was one man whose example set my standards for book production and scholarship throughout those years it was Stanley Morison. In 1928, when I first met him, he was a powerful figure in the Monotype Corporation. It was Eric Gill who suggested that I should meet him, as I had just begun to get *Order* under way and needed advice on typography and format. Morison (I call him thus because he always shrank from Christian names, maybe from some egalitarian itch) was at the head and heart of a veritable revolution in typography and Eric was charged with designing new type faces.

In response to my tentative approach Morison asked me to lunch at the Holborn Restaurant. I was confronted by a tall thin stooping figure in a black suit, white shirt and black tie. He never dressed otherwise except when he donned an incongruous seersucker for the occasional heatwave in London or New York. Sharp eyes glared through thick spectacles. There was an ominous frown on his face which broke up with a friendly grin, like the sun coming through thunder-clouds.

He listened attentively as I sketched my ideas about a policy for *Order*. Then suddenly broke in: 'I suppose you think that you're *orthodox*.' I tried to explain that my kind of dissidence was indeed compatible with orthodoxy. With many a growl he then proceeded to expound his own views about the Church. They seemed to be far more critical than my own. 'But if those are your views, Mr Morison, why do you stay in the Roman Church?' At this point he banged the table so hard that everything rattled: 'Stay in it? I wouldn't stay with that bunch of macaroni merchants [another bang] another minute if it wasn't the only way of laying hold on Christ.' His cry had brought the entire restaurant to a brief silence; it became embedded in my very being thereafter.

It was the beginning of a close friendship which lasted until his death in 1967. He was my senior by seventeen years and a master in so many ways where I was an enthusiastic novice. My admiration and affection went hand in hand.

In 1913 Morison had been an employee of Burns & Oates, helping Francis Meynell with that publisher's exceptionally high standard of book production. He once told me that he had earned extra money by addressing envelopes far into the night. This had enabled him to go to Bruges, to a Benedictine monastery nearby, to hear plainchant, which became his abiding passion. From the humblest origins, with an atheist background, he had come eventually to seek instruction in the Catholic faith at Farm Street church. 'The priest smelt of port,' he recalled, but the new wine of the Gospel had taken a hold on him which was never relaxed. It could be said that he was deeply religious but would be driven into a frenzy of indignation, for instance, about the anti-Modernist papal encyclical. 'How *can* they go on saying that Moses wrote the Pentateuch?' Happily he was very friendly with two remarkable scholar-priests with whom he would confer on 'where the shoe pinches', as he would say: Adrian Fortescue and Herbert Thurston, SJ, the one a liturgist, the other a tireless and indeed peerless debunker of bad history and bogus expressions of religion.

I never knew a man with such a wide range of friendships as Morison. His stretched from Robert Bridges, the Poet Laureate, to Beaverbrook, the newspaper tycoon, but he preferred seeing them separately; and only a discernible group, such as typographers, would also know each other. He loved the corridors of power, especially when they led to the dining-room. He was the true ascetic: one who thoroughly appreciates the good things of life. He was careless and generous about money. When I first met him I was comparatively poor. 'But don't you worry about *money*, go for *power* and you won't be able to stop the stuff coming in,' he once told me.

After the war, when I had moved to Burns & Oates, we would try so to arrange it that my annual visit to the United States coincided with one of his more frequent trips. We travelled together on board the *Queen Mary* or the *Queen Elizabeth*. He liked the discreet grill room on the upper deck and would engage the wine steward in long disputation before making his choice. (In my pre-war Sheed & Ward days I perforce travelled in the humbler tourist class, with its warm companionship. On one such trip I found Fr D'Arcy there and had to serve him early morning Mass each day after a night of revelry, a test of faith and friendship if ever there was one.)

In due course Morison became an *eminence grise* at *The Times*, writing its history and designing its new typeface and layout. He also redesigned *The Times Literary Supplement* and became increasingly critical of its editorial policy. Finally, on the resignation of the editor, he was given the chair himself and ran the paper with success for a couple of years before getting his chosen candidate, Alan Pryce-Jones, to succeed him.

I recall a very happy day with the two of them. Alan wanted to salute the man who, under God, had instructed him in the faith, Fr C. C. Martindale, SJ, then in his old age and put out to grass in the Jesuit retirement home near Petworth in Sussex. In characteristic style Alan hired a Rolls-Royce, Morison produced champagne which we consumed by the roadside, and our guest was wafted to a nearby hostelry for luncheon. It was one of those English summer days that lingers in the memory when it coincides with some special occasion. Each of us had different debts of gratitude to pay to a quintessential Jesuit priest: it was pilgrimage with a purpose.

At Sheed & Ward Morison had been my model with his innovative simplicities of type and layout. Our gap in mutual understanding was his Victor Gollancz and Left Book Club connection. How logical and how boring was the mechanistic Marxism which forced all Gollancz productions into black binding and yellow covers!

We were much more at home together at Burns & Oates. He brought me into contact with Brooke Crutchley and the Cambridge University Press. Brooke was a superb technician and when it came to liturgical printing his Catholic background gave him an added incentive to produce the exactly adequate medium for the text. I had short notice of the Catholic celebration of the coronation of the Queen in 1953. Brooke produced the perfect production – a rubricated thirty-two page pamphlet which sold 100,000 copies on publication.

So I leave Morison, splendid artificer, counsellor, friend. In his later days he realised that he was slowly going blind and bought himself an elaborate stereo and a pack of Gregorian chant records. He made meticulous arrangements for the liturgy of his Requiem at Westminster Cathedral and in this way went out with dignity into the world of light.

★   ★   ★

With Morison and Alan Pryce-Jones, I had saluted Fr C. C. Martindale on that happy day in Sussex. Similar memories attend my friendship with Fr Martin D'Arcy, who had taught Henry and me at Stonyhurst and went on to considerable fame and status. His rise in the Church was rapid, culminating in the post of Provincial of the English Jesuit Province in 1945, but was then followed by a long descent into disillusion and disappointment.

His influence on me at Stonyhurst had, of course, been great and I cannot say that the tables were turned when I became his publisher, but certainly my editing was necessary and extensive as he always wrote against time and with many distractions. As Master of Campion Hall, Oxford (1933–1945), he became an almost legendary figure, commissioning a fine new building from Sir Edwin Lutyens, presiding over a hospitable High Table, attracting some of the most brilliant young minds of the university with consequent conversions. He was unashamedly an elitist, a traditionalist (except for a pioneering spirit in his philosophical thought); he had a romantic vision of a past which perhaps never existed. Although he was a strict ascetic in his personal life he was indulgent towards those who certainly were far from being so. He took good-natured teasing about his views and foibles from those, like myself, who were indulged in this way. When he became Provincial his grandiose scheme for a sort of renaissance of the Jesuit province in acquiring stately homes for its centres and the like, fell foul with his superiors in Rome and he was summarily demoted. He took it hard but found fresh scope for his abilities in the United States where his lectures were in wide demand and new friends abounded. A man of less holiness would have become embittered but he survived some twenty-five years with a resolute mind – even if, in his last years, a closed one. He was grateful for the hospitality of his old friends and – heaven knows – they had cause to be grateful to him. He died in 1976 at the age of eighty-eight.

Martin D'Arcy was a high-flyer, as were Ronald Knox and David Knowles, to mention a few at random – men known to the general public. Of course, I knew many other priests, less well known and too many to recall here except as a fairly representative selection.

There was Fr Vassall-Philips, a hangover, surely, from the Oxford Movement. An elderly gentleman but energetic in mind and body, very handsome, eyes like a tropical blue sky, he was a gentle controversialist in his books and at Speaker's Corner in Hyde Park. There, in a weather-worn habit of the Redemptorist Order with a vast rosary dangling from his waist, his earnestness and simplicity kept the crowd quiet. He had a sense of eternity but no sense of time and would drop into my office just for a chat for half an hour or so that I could ill afford. He was by no means the only one.

In total contrast was Fr Philip Hughes, a sharp mind from Liverpool, a specialist in Reformation history but also a liberal interpreter of Church history generally. He had no support, financial or otherwise, from the hierarchy or any academic institution – moving from a bed-sitter to the Reading Room of the British Museum with dogged perseverance. He was a man after Stanley Morison's heart for his integrity. I was delighted when he accepted a chair at Notre-Dame University, Indiana, where he ended his days with his merits recognised at last.

Gerald Vann was a Dominican in the vintage years of that ancient order in England under Bede Jarret and including John-Baptist Reeves and Thomas Gilby who were putting Thomism back on the map. Gerald was small, incandescent, quiet, with a surprisingly deep voice. Aldous Huxley greatly respected him as I noticed when we all met together. He brought a new note into spiritual writing. He died early of cancer, carrying on to the last, even grateful for a large whisky, collapsing on a sofa at home from exhaustion.

Tom Corbishly, Jesuit, was a latecomer, when he was Master of Campion Hall and later Superior at Farm Street. He was a great ecumenist, preached in Westminster Abbey and got into hot water from Cardinal Heenan for con-celebrating with an Anglican, but he was a sound theologian and a valued adviser at some crucial points during my editorship of *The Tablet*, notably when I took a stand against the Pope's encyclical on birth control.

A much older Jesuit was Herbert Thurston who had been a friend of his fellow Jesuit, George Tyrell. His immense learning was largely hidden in back numbers of *The Month*, famous for its soporific effect at that time. ('I feel very sleepy, there must be a copy of *The Month* in the room,' once drawled a friend of mine.) Thurston's own essays were far from characteristic of the journal; he concentrated on debunking dubious legends of the saints, hysterical visionaries, bogus 'miracles' and spiritualism (an impertinent young Jesuit once asked him, 'Father, is it all right if I believe in the Trinity?'). But he was a great believer *au fond*, probably the reason why Stanley Morison was attracted to his views. I collected his essays in several books with a modest success.

Of Canon Francis Bartlett who died in March 1992 I quote a brief notice which I wrote for the *Bulletin* of Westminster Cathedral at the editor's request. I called it 'The Last Biretta'.

My title comes from a vivid recollection of Francis Bartlett, in the Cathedral or in the precincts; a tall, gaunt figure with a soutane down to his ankles, sometimes with a great black cloak flung over his shoulders, crowned with a battered biretta worn at a rakish angle. There was an Edwardian air about him, although he wasn't as old as all that, when I first met him, forty years ago. There was a whiff of St Sulpice in Paris, his old seminary, about him; a hint also of St Peter's piazza in Rome; everywhere he had a certain panache.

The biretta was part of it and its like is hardly ever seen in Church today. It is difficult to explain how such a special and private person – not a public figure and not a preacher or writer of renown – should have attracted so much attention in the obituary columns of the national press and even in a trendy magazine like *Oldie*. He spent thirty years of his priesthood at Westminster Cathedral, where he was Administrator for ten years; most of his childhood was passed in the Cathedral precincts, his godfather was Cardinal Bourne.

He was indeed a living part of that magnificent edifice. It is to be hoped that there will be at least a plaque in his memory. No wonder the Cathedral was full of friends at his requiem, that some thirty priests, several bishops and Cardinal Hume concelebrated his requiem Mass.

The secret of his success was his gift for friendship, which is the art of self-giving. He would go out of himself, as it were, to share the interests, the happiness, the anxiety or the tragedy in the lives of those whom he met. And he met a great many people because his interests were so wide. The way of the world fascinated him in a detached sort of way; he was indulgent about its follies, appreciative of its achievements. His art, more than a hobby, was photography and he had a special eye for beauty in unexpected places. All this exuberance was stilled, distilled, in the quiet intensity and disciplined grace of his way of saying Mass. He was first and last a priest.

Finally John McCormack, a Mill Hill missionary. He was a highly-qualified demographer and had seen the unbridled fecundity of the human race at close quarters in many parts of the world. His efforts on the Justice and Peace Commission in Rome were unavailing, his one-man Population Centre cold-shouldered. I was glad to use his knowledge in *The Tablet* for many years to our mutual encouragement, as his population warning got through.

There may be a typical parson, there is no such thing as a typical priest. Their only common denominator seems to me to be abnegation, although their infinitely varied characters and talents obscured this negative note, if it is one. They had a charisma in common, a knowledge of human nature which excluded any censorious tendency, they were classless and never trendy: the salt of the earth.

12

Editor of *The Tablet*

In *The Tablet* of 4 February 1967 an announcement appeared, discreetly 'boxed' at the tail-end of the paper, to the effect that Douglas Woodruff would be retiring at the end of April after thirty-one years of editorship and that I would be his successor, 'having been associated with *The Tablet* during the whole period of the present editorship and closely acquainted with all sides of the paper'. The statement seemed to imply, what doubtless its author sought to enjoin, a smooth continuity of editorial policy. While this was true as far as it went, it did not go far enough and wholly misrepresented the facts. Thirty years on and I was a different person, the world a different place, and the Church itself had undergone a mutation at the Vatican Council. To put all this into perspective I must encapsulate the paper's situation from the time of the takeover in 1936 to my own taking it over in 1965. (The story is told in detail in Michael Walsh's book, *The Tablet, 1840–1990*, published on the occasion of the paper's hundred and fiftieth anniversary.)

Cardinal Hinsley, an old man but a brisk new broom as Archbishop of Westminster, had decided to restore the paper to the lay ownership of its origins which had lasted for twenty-eight years. In 1936 he approached Douglas Woodruff as the prospective editor. Douglas had a formidable track record for the job: at Oxford a Lothian prize-winner, a first in history and President of the Union, and at the time a leader-writer for *The Times*. He knew everybody in the English Catholic establishment. He was married to Mia Acton, an altogether splendid person and the granddaughter of the legendary historian. Neither

shared Lord Acton's liberal views. Ecclesiastically Douglas was a
safe pair of hands. He had all the qualifications for a chairman-
editor except an essential one: a capacity for organisation.

He approached me when the whole scheme was no more than
a gleam in his eye and happily I was able to get it into shape.

I was with Longmans at the time and persuaded them to house
the paper in their spacious offices, for prestige and as a boost for
the Catholic side of their publishing. Longmans, at my suggestion, also bought non-voting shares. I had to deal with many
complications in the transfer, appoint a new lawyer and
accountants and so forth. Happily I was known to the cardinal's
solicitors which helped considerably. My record, as the editor of
Order, of intransigent hostility towards the policies of the
outgoing editor of *The Tablet* was quietly passed over.

As Douglas left most matters of administration to me, so I left
all editorial matters to him and kept my distance from them
except on rare occasions when I had to stand in for him when he
went abroad or was ill.

In my view he was not a great editor but as a leader-writer he
was beyond compare. He would fill the front three or four pages
with a *tour d'horizon* of world affairs, viewed through his own
lenses but with a sagacity and fund of knowledge unsurpassed in
the secular weeklies. The rest of the paper would come together
almost by accident. 'Who are the little men who write the rest of
the paper for you?' Evelyn Waugh would ask him in his teasing
inquisitive manner. Effectively *The Tablet* became 'D.W.'s
Weekly' and even so gained an impressive reputation with the
media.

In the last years of his editorship, which lasted through
Vatican II, it failed to represent the emergent Church. Moreover
I was dismayed to discover, through a questionnaire addressed to
subscribers, that their average age was over seventy years. 'It's
an elephant dying on its feet,' I protested to Douglas. As editor-
elect I made no secret of my determination to change its whole
outlook. I circulated a memo to the holdings board of which *The
Tablet* was by this time a subsidiary. I quote a few paragraphs to

show something of my views at that time (thirty years after the takeover):

> *The Tablet*'s responsibility and its potential influence are greater at this time than at any other in its hundred years of history. If Catholicism in England has emerged from the ghetto, this must not suggest a merger with the surrounding world. Ecumenism is not the last refuge of feeble ecclesiastical minds but a gathering of strength from all the sources and resources of Christian values in face of the ultimate challenge of atheism, in all its expressions in personal and political life.
>
> It is in the matter of this emergence and this ecumenism that *The Tablet* can now play a leading part. Its new impetus must be, indeed, that of the Church herself as a result of Vatican II. The Church has come to a new self-consciousness; a fresh view of her nature, purpose, and appropriate manner of life.
>
> Without pushing paradox too far, it might be said that whereas it has been the common view hitherto that a human being makes an act of faith in the Church for the solution of his problems, the Church now makes an act of faith in her own people for the fulfilment of her mission. Human intelligence and conscience are now to be trusted with a wider range and responsibility in the apostolate of word and deed, not necessarily dependent on ecclesiastical status.
>
> It is not a question now of particular social or economic systems, or political views, or philosophical and scientific disciplines, or literary and aesthetic criteria coming under the ban or the blessing of the supreme authority. (History shows both the evil and/or the ineffectiveness of ecclesiastical pretensions in these matters.) It is a question of the individual examining any of these with rational freedom, judging on intrinsic merit, alerted by a grace-enlightened sense of values. The nature, claims and limits of authority must be observed, a sense of expediency ever-present, but the opportunity of extending the kingdom of God within and without is essentially an individual matter.
>
> This journal is committed to Christian optimism in seeing humanity as in progress towards fulfilment but it is not triumphalist in terms of Catholic statistics. Where preaching is concerned, it is important to preach to the converted. Formal heresy is rare, material heresy is everywhere and by no means confined to 'our separated brethren'. This journal will forward and follow every move of the Church towards purifying dogma from its excrescences.

Editor of The Tablet *(1967–82)*

Publisher to the Holy See: with (c. 1960) Pope Paul VI

Editor of The Tablet: *audience in Rome with (c. 1980) Pope John Paul II*

This manifesto was judged to be a recipe for disaster by some of my colleagues, and Douglas worked assiduously and secretly to reverse the decision about my appointment which had been made long since.

Two concepts were now in open confrontation. Douglas had his vision of the Church as a complete society, Vatican-based, with all the answers for an unheeding world. In my own reading I had studied the German Jesuit theologian Karl Rahner and his French equivalent Henri de Lubac. They were leading figures in reversing the whole trend of Vatican II away from the blueprint produced by the Roman Curia. Douglas did not appreciate the thrust and direction of the Council whilst it was in session and minimised the final outcome. He held that it would take the Church a hundred years to recover from it. My own view was totally opposed. I stuck to my guns and reinforced my position by finding generous friends to provide sufficient working capital to see the paper safe for a few years.

This parting of the ways saddened me but we renewed our friendship in his last years. I formed a new Board and invited him to join it but he was by then a sick man and gave me never a word of encouragement or approbation. It is difficult to dry-out resentment in the soul.

In the months between my leaving Burns & Oates and taking over *The Tablet* there was mounting pressure in the Church for a revision of its birth control ruling. I realised that this was not just an isolated matter but would have the widest repercussions, involving the authority not only of the Pope but of all the gradations of authority which went under the blanket term, the *magisterium*.

The Pope had withheld the whole question from discussion in the Council itself. It may have been a prudent move because the virtual unanimity of the bishops on most matters of doctrine and discipline would undoubtedly have split on this one. I had talks with Third World bishops at the Council who saw no problem in big families, blandly regarding them as essential in their local, social and economic habits and structures, quite apart from doctrinal considerations. But I knew more than one member of the papal Commission which had been set up by Pope John and augmented by Pope Paul and felt sure that it would come up with a conclusion contrary to the current teaching. This view was supported by reports of many specialised congresses abroad and the pastoral utterances of a number of European bishops. The letter columns of *The Tablet* were nearly all in favour of reform. All this despite the fact that for years the subject had been totally taboo in official Catholic circles. A wide-ranging Gallup Poll, confined to practising Catholics, published by *The Daily Telegraph* in March 1967, revealed that no less than 62 per cent thought that 'there could be good reasons for contraceptive methods of birth control in marriage'.

A few weeks later I was sent anonymously, from the United States, a translation of the actual findings of the Commission, which were strictly secret at the time. The Kansas City postmark suggested the *National Catholic Reporter* as the sender. I rang up the editor, an old friend, and he confirmed that he had sent the document, had commissioned its translation from the Latin original and was about to publish. This relieved me from any qualms about confidentiality and I decided to go ahead.

The report was a bombshell, recommending as it did a total modification of the traditional teaching. Rome authenticated the document but condemned its unauthorised publication and said that the current ruling must hold until such a time as the Pope gave his own final word. Many Catholics, following the dictum of St Augustine – *in dublis libertas* – decided that there was indeed freedom in an area of doubt. *Humanae Vitae* was to follow eighteen months later.

Meanwhile I surveyed my new little empire. I was not only editor but virtually proprietor. It was hard going. I found a small and disaffected staff, poor premises and no working capital to speak of. But I knew that I could count on the moral support of those readers who shared my enthusiasm for all that Vatican II implied and that they would support me at any time of financial crisis. This they did generously in response to my urgent appeal for funds to meet a steep rise in the cost of paper and print.

From the start I wanted the renewal of *The Tablet* to be not an individual but a communal effort. I was fortunate in the number of friends, clerical and lay, who came to my help with their specialised knowledge and their pioneering views. I saw the role of editor as that of the conductor of an orchestra. I started a monthly dining club in a local pub for an inner circle of collaborators: it grew and grew, ran successfully throughout my editorship and goes on to this day. We had a Mass in the crypt of Westminster Cathedral before the dinner – not obligatory but well attended. I could not separate the work from prayer and indeed thought these two could be synonymous: *laborare est orare* was simply a truism. Prayer as petition, as meditation, or as a liturgical act are valid concepts, but prayer as the right and normal exercise of one's being is not so generally recognised. 'One can pray very well when one is fast asleep,' Abbot Chapman of Downside had remarked to me once. 'The just man justices; keeps grace; that keeps all his goings graces;' wrote Hopkins. To me this was what religion was all about: a link, a relationship, an acknowledged dependence on God. It might imply, it certainly did not enforce, a state of personal holiness. That can follow. Recognition of our state of dependence is the thing: one can grow up from that. Of course it is not a steady progress: 'God writes straight with crooked lines', as Teresa of Avila once observed.

Apart from the birth control question, the other great preoccupation of *The Tablet* readers, I discovered, was the reform of the liturgy, and the use of the vernacular: two separate matters but constantly confused. With a radicalism which nobody expected, the Tridentine Mass was declared obsolete and was substituted by a text deemed to be more suited, liturgically and historically, to the significance of the Sacrifice.

The decree was welcomed by the Church as a whole but brought dismay and desolation to devotees of the old Mass throughout the world. In England they appealed to *The Tablet* as the only forum for responsible discussion. The world at large stood amazed at the heartfelt fervour, the depth of learning and the sheer misery displayed by liturgists, poets and plain people at the changes.

I also was surprised. Many writers were close personal friends – all spoke from the heart. My heart spoke otherwise. I was wholly familiar, of course, with the superb architecture of the Tridentine Mass. I was aware of its mounting drama from the prayers at the foot of the altar to the triumphant coda of the last Gospel. No ballet or opera could compete with this compelling structure. All the great composers had taken it as a basis for their work; no language was adequate but the Latin – timeless, with a restrained eloquence and exactitude that made it a supreme work of art. All this I realised, but there was something more: the very act needed to be expressed in our own terms, those of our limitations, our condition, the humanity of our day. Traditional-ists had imputed to Latin not only the poetry, which it plainly possessed, a music of its own, but the quality of an incantation: a relation of word and deed; a verbal formula for producing a change, a sort of alchemy. The medium was in danger of becoming the message.

The change of rhythm from book publishing to editing a weekly was total. Most books have a gestation period from manuscript to publication of nine months or so. It now gave a new sense of achievement to see what I had written or commissioned appear within a few days. I welcomed the problems and decisions that faced me every morning, the deadlines and the constant contact with writers and readers. Editing is a drug, a stimulant that few

men relinquish willingly. There is, of course, an additional
dimension to the editing of a Catholic paper; its outlook cannot
be just pragmatic. Hardly a year passes without some major
preoccupation needing more than political vision. Here I recall
just a few in my fifteen years.

Since 1967 the war in Nigeria had been regarded specially by
Catholics as a pitiless onslaught against the partly Catholic Ibo
tribe by the Islamic and pagan forces of the Federal Government.
The Pope in a public address had deplored the plight of the Ibos.
Cardinal Heenan, on the rare occasion of a sermon preached in
Westminster Abbey, had rhetorically asked why there had been
no marches and demonstrations in London in support of the Ibos.
Novelists such as Graham Greene, Muriel Spark and Auberon
Waugh had taken up their cause. I was besieged by Irish
missionaries from the region with tales of genocide and the most
grisly photographs. But I had my doubts. My exceptionally well-
placed and balanced correspondent in Lagos was steadily telling
me a different story.

Suddenly an opportunity opened to get at the truth. I had a
surprise visit from Sir Adetokumbo Ademola, Chief Justice of
Nigeria, who was in London on business connected with the
International Red Cross, of which he was the Nigerian president.
It would be hard to imagine a man less swayed by partisan
emotions. He was a Catholic and quite appalled by what he
described as a caricature of the situation as presented to
European Catholics. It was greatly endangering the Church in
Nigeria. He asked me if I would accept an invitation from his
government to see things for myself. I could travel wherever I
wanted, talk to anyone, fix my own route. I accepted and he was
as good as his word. On 1 November 1968 I flew to Lagos, a car
and a courier were at my disposal, the Nigerian Government
serving only to provide transport by air and road and to arrange
a number of official meetings.

Catholic contacts were quickly organised by the bishops'
secretaries at Lagos, and I met missionaries in the most remote
places as well as close to the actual restricted scene of battle.

'Civil war' conveys the idea of a nation divided, but as far as this uprising was concerned it was limited to one-tenth of one state where between 3 million and 4 million of the Ibo population was concentrated – out of 55 million of various tribes in the country as a whole, which was at peace. From Lagos I travelled westwards to Ibadan, east to Calabar, north to Kano and Kaduna. I was welcomed by bishops and missonaries, doctors, nursing sisters and schoolteachers. Wherever I went I talked to soldiers in hospital and near the front line, and with the military commanders of three regions. I saw much of the ubiquitous international observers from the United Nations whose journeys often coincided with my own. They made an impressive team consisting of major-generals from Canada and Sweden, a Polish colonel and the colourful Brigadier Bernard Fergusson of Chindit fame. We shared the sparse but efficient hospitality of various government rest-houses scattered about the country and often exchanged information. The coincidence of this official tour with my own was a godsend and confirmed all that I had myself observed.

I wrote a detailed report for *The Tablet* (7 and 14 December 1968). My recollections of my visit to General Gowon, the head of state and commander-in-chief of the Federal army, were written at the time.

> I wondered what sort of man he was ... The meeting lasted for an hour and a half and was wholly informal. There were no prepared questions or stereotyped answers. It ended with a casual stroll round his quarters, the general opening his Cabinet room with his own key, dropping in at the squash court to watch a game, and giving a friendly goodbye wave at the gate. There was a touch of Sandhurst in his vocabulary. The overall impression was one of transparent honesty, of an integrated personality ...
>
> I came to realise that he regards himself simply as a soldier called to the service of his country, longing for its peace and stability and ready to quit when both were assured; that his dedication was unequivocally based on his view of Christian living. Life would be meaningless for him without vocation. He takes as much for granted in his own government, and in fact ticked off on a list, for my benefit,

the religious allegiance of each member, Christian or Moslem. The former preponderate, with Catholics much in evidence. The proportion is unimportant. What struck me was his assumption that a man should have some form of religious belief, and the fact that his broadly based government pulled together for one Nigeria, against tribalism or any form of separatism. He had, he told me, carried this principle through all ranks of his army, so that no unit was synonymous with a tribal group.

It would be difficult to imagine a man more fitted by birth and circumtance for bringing a united Nigeria into the community of nations. By race and region, by training and creed, he is at once radically Nigerian and open to the Western world. His family, of a minor tribe, comes from the centre of the country. His father was a Church Missionary Society evangelist whose work took him to Zaria, in the north central state, a largely Moslem area. Yakubu Gowon was born in a village nearby at Wusasa and had his schooling there, before going into the army in 1954. His officer training was in England: he was at Eaton Hall and Sandhurst, and at the Joint Services Staff College.

For General Gowon, the outcome of the war was a foregone conclusion. His only question was why it should have begun. The record stands, of his conciliatory attitudes and almost excessive toleration of the growing demands of his one-time friend and fellow-officer Ojukwu. He recalled these, and his further attempts at peace-making after the outbreak, with an air almost of incredulity that such ambition and malice should have possessed this man. 'Honestly, who would have thought it?' The only trace of indignation was when it came to recounting how Colonel Ojukwu had come to use his religion for purposes of propaganda. Nigeria has traditionally been the most tolerant of countries in this matter: Christian, Moslem and pagan were often to be found living under one roof. As the general saw it, Colonel Ojukwu was now endangering this balance. He is a Catholic by baptism (though notoriously detached in observance) and had chosen to use his religion as a rallying-cry for resistance and an appeal to the outside world.

General Gowon assured me that freedom for the Christian churches would continue after the war. It had been so before, and I was a witness of the missionary return to territory liberated from the rebel troops ...

Learning that I was to fly next day to Kano and travel by road to Kaduna, he said that I must stop by Zaria and visit his home nearby. 'The house was almost *too* close to the church for me as a boy, but you'll see for yourself.' I followed his suggestion and enquired for his father at the admirable CMS hospital at Wusasa. He lives in a house in the village street, fronting a small-holding ... The houses are gathered round the village church – a very simple building, with beautiful lines, of reinforced mud. The General's father is an old man of great courtesy and charm who cannot remember how many years he has lived – he suggests 90: a happy man with his small crops and poultry, living in total simplicity. He has little to spare, but he gave me a large bunch of bananas as a parting gift. For him his fifth child, the Head of State, was, he reckoned, 'a good son'.

An unforgettable impression was of a big hospital at Uyo, a catchment area for children left starving by the passage of war. There were four large wards, the first for practically hopeless cases, where listless little ones with swollen bellies and matchstick limbs spoke only with their eyes, which had sunk into their heads. Injections and spoon-feeding would save some of them and, as they came back to life, they were moved to the next ward and a different diet. Here they gradually recovered and could be moved on to the third ward, on normal diet. The fourth ward was more like a playroom than anything else; here the children came up smiling, here they romped and chattered regardless of tribe or of what side they came from. Thus, I hoped, would the country come to itself again.

After more than three weeks of ceaseless movement I was dumped on the tarmac of Kano airport by the ramshackle aircraft of a local line. Here the Alitalia flight to Rome was waiting to take off. I scrambled aboard at the last minute. My aspect must have been unusual since an air-hostess immediately produced a whisky-and-soda without being asked.

In Rome the British Embassy arranged for me to see Cardinal Casaroli, the Vatican Secretary of State. That sagacious diplomat listened to my plea for a shift in Vatican policy and a better understanding of General Gowon's position. Happily my visit coincided with that of the bishops from Nigeria making the same protest and plea – and it was not without effect.

★   ★   ★

I suppose that never in the 150 years of the paper's existence has an editor of *The Tablet* been presented with a problem of conscience and policy so grave as that which confronted me with the publication of *Humanae Vitae*, the Pope's final word on birth control. Eighteen months earlier *The Tablet*'s publishing of the Commission's secret report had produced a furore. The matter had effectively been thrown open to debate and all views were allowable. Now that the Pope had uttered, the case was altered. The Vatican press office hastened to say it was a non-infallible document. Nevertheless the full weight of the *magisterium* was behind it and all bishops were bound to follow its teaching.

I sought some qualified theological advice and was confirmed in my view that I must oppose the encyclical. Although it frequently quoted the Council's decree, *Gaudium et spes*, I wrote, neither joy nor hope could be derived from reading it. The Pope had overridden his own commission of specialists as well as widespread theological opinion. In doing so he had opened a sombre chapter in the history of the Church where authority would be subject to questions from all directions. So I wrote: nothing more than a statement of fact. I had no word of reproof from Cardinal Heenan or any other authority in the Church. Bishop Butler, a learned historical theologian, later told me that the encyclical had not been 'received' by the Church, which fact invalidated it, he said.

But another learned Benedictine, David Knowles, the Regius Professor of Modern History at Cambridge and a very old friend, took a different view. He had telephoned me towards midnight on the night before *The Tablet* was due to go to press. 'I hope you are not going to attack the Pope,' he said solemnly.

'Yes, I'm afraid I am; there's nothing else I can do in conscience.'

There followed a chat when I reminded him as a historian of the many examples of fallibility and worse in papal history. Later I invited him to express his views in *The Tablet* which I printed under the title, '*Audi alteram partem*'. There was an unedifying sequel to this: the *Osservatore Romano*, which had assiduously quoted any favourable opinion in the world press, had, of course, omitted *The Tablet*'s view. Now, without permission, it splashed across its front page David Knowles's article under a banner headline, '*The Tablet* supports *Humanae Vitae*'.

My view was endorsed months later over a *tête-à-tête* dinner at the Garrick with the Cardinal-Archbishop of Washington: '*Humanae Vitae* is a dead letter, Tom.' Cardinal Baum's view was that of perhaps the majority of bishops in the Western Church. I found these contradictions between their private views and public stance dismaying. But I now realise that the encyclical has a 'prophetic' quality above and beyond its language, pointing to an ideal which must be safeguarded against the world's purely hedonistic view. This is what the bishops defend – although it must be said that the encyclical drafted by the Pope's Commission has a more realistic pastoral approach.

The birth control crisis was the greatest challenge that came my way. It has now evaporated to some extent: Catholics at large have given their judgement. The question is now in the forum of individual conscience.

★   ★   ★

Meanwhile on the week-by-week running of the paper I was like a busy gardener; pruning here, weeding there, planting and doing my best to enrich the soil. I had the most willing help from so many friends in a position to know more than I did about any special subject. They worked for nominal payment in those days of financial hardship, as did my new staff. There were many innovations; a favourite for many readers has been 'The Living Spirit', a column of extracts from spiritual writers of all centuries. I wanted this personal religion to balance a surfeit of ecclesiasticism. 'Periscope' and 'In the margin' were boxed features for views not necessarily those of the paper. Similarly 'Pastor Ignotus', a role filled by a succession of parish priests, voiced parish problems. I was delighted to watch the Letters column grow so that it became an exchange for the varieties of Catholic opinion. I saw that *The Tablet* always had the inside edge against other journals of opinion. They largely ignored what to my mind is the most important element in human affairs: the religious.

I decided to change the policy of the paper on two major matters, Ireland and Israel. My predecessor was generally unsympathetic to both. I decided to work towards reconciliation in Ireland. In many visits to Dublin and Belfast I discovered little-known groups working for mutual understanding and peace. Billy Clonmore (of my Sheed & Ward days), now Lord Wicklow, and his wife, Eleanor Butler (the daughter of a famous painter), were tireless in these areas. Garret Fitzgerald in Dublin and John Hume, head of the SDLP in Belfast, were specially helpful. I had met many of the journalists in Rome in the days of Vatican II and found them more than willing to write for the annual Irish issue which I published each year on St Patrick's Day. Of great help was Louis McRedmond, then one of the heads of Irish Television, who became *The Tablet*'s regular Dublin correspondent. Through Basil Clancy I was invited with my wife to meet Eamon de Valera in his last year of office (1973). He had an air of greatness about him and I was amused to see the old revolutionary's Spanish origins emerge as my wife talked to him. Later I met Jack Lynch, prime minister at the time, who was particularly keen that I should intensify my policy.

The higher clergy were a different matter: the stern Mgr McQuaid, the puritanical Archbishop of Dublin (who had protested at lingerie being displayed in shop windows) was a cold but courteous host, as also was Bishop Philbin of Belfast (adamant about segregated schools which, to me, were at the root of sectarian conflict). The head of Maynooth, which had almost the monopoly of clerical training, and later the primate of the Irish hierarchy, was lavish in his hospitality but he was possessed of a fierce nationalism with a scarcely concealed dislike of England. As a result of all these contacts *The Tablet* has penetrated into areas where it had been boycotted for generations.

★ ★ ★

Israel, of course, was quite a different problem. Douglas always showed signs of a Bellocian strain of anti-Semitism, or at best his was a negative attitude. He did not regard Judaism as the vital prophet, precursor and essential ingredient of Christianity, as I had always seen it to be.

It struck me that *The Tablet* should adopt a policy of looking for common ground with the Jewish faith. The change was noticed in Jewish circles. I was frequently the guest at the British-Israel society lunches where I had the opportunity of good talk with men like Herzog, now the President of Israel, and Kollak, the Mayor of Jerusalem. The Israeli ambassador at the time, a charming and highly intelligent man, asked me to lunch at the Athenaeum and we had a wide-ranging talk. A few days later he was brutally shot down by Arab terrorists in Park Lane. Israel's hardening attitude and the position of the persecuted Palestinians made it difficult to build bridges at the political level but I had at least provided an opportunity for a small degree of mutual understanding on all-important matters of religion.

Apart from the Nigerian experience there were two other big breaks in my editing routine. One sprang from the Polish organisation called Pax which invited me to Poland in 1970. Pax was Catholic but had made its separate peace with the Communist regime. It consisted of entrepreneurs, publicists and some collaborating priests. It was condemned by the Polish hierarchy but thrived under State protection. It was impossible for a journalist to get a visa for Poland without the authority of Pax which also did its best to shadow and shape a journalist's trip. But to the editor of *The Tablet* it was specially benevolent: apart from an official dinner and talk with its representatives, I was left almost at liberty. A book could be written about its sinister founder, Piasecki, but his son invited me to his home and presented me to his delightful wife and family. My real purpose was to see an old Polish friend, Jerzy Turowicz, the editor of *Znak*, roughly the equivalent of *The Tablet*, but of course censored and persecuted, mainly by having its paper ration cut to the minimum. Jerzy, a man of faith and great moral courage, invited me to his home in Cracow. Pax raised no objection but suggested that an interpreter should accompany me. I had no need of one as Jerzy was fluent in English. So I flew off alone and was greeted at the airport by him and his friends.

He suggested a visit to Auschwitz, the German concentration camp of infamous memory. It is kept intact by the Poles as a memorial to the countless dead – Jews for the most part but also resistant Catholics who were also murdered there in cold blood. The visit was a descent into Hell. There were row after row of big wooden huts between asphalted paths which might have been a military camp on Salisbury Plain. The facade hid a reality which stunned one with its evil implications. Some huts were crammed to the roof with tiers of narrow wooden bunks, so close to each other that there would be only just enough room to lie down. Then there were storerooms where were piled the battered suitcases of those who must have once thought that they had a journey and a new home ahead. Another storeroom was for human hair – a tangled mass of many colours. A larger hut, without windows, was the gas chamber, next door to the incinerator. There was an execution yard, its further wall pock-marked with bullet holes. Nearby there were punishment cells where a man could neither stand up nor lie full length. Here Fr Kolbe, a Polish priest, had been confined for three days without food or water before being shot. His crime had been to offer to substitute himself for a prisoner about to face the firing squad who pleaded that he had a wife and little children. His offer was accepted with this extra punishment thrown in. I was speechless as I walked round the place with Jerzy and his friends. We were almost alone and each of us retreated into our inner selves, finding it impossible to communicate our desolation. To add to it, I was told that there was a similar camp for women nearby.

Later we came into the great square at the heart of Cracow. Over some flagstones fresh flowers had been scattered; it was the spot where a Polish student had immolated himself in protest at the German occupation. The flowers are still renewed daily. As we stood there Cardinal Woytila crossed the square coming towards us. 'We are being followed, I can't introduce you,' Jerzy whispered hurriedly. Cardinal Woytila passed with a brief smile for my host. I was not to talk to him until much later when his black *soutane* had given place to a white one – the uniform of only one man in the world.

Back in Warsaw I saw little of my official hosts but a good deal of the *Financial Times* correspondent, Chris Bobinski, and his circle of mostly younger university people. How they kept their gaiety, what original and comfy little homes they had made for themselves in the forbidding Communist-style blocks of flats that had been built over the ruins of Warsaw, convinced me that the spirit of Poland was inextinguishable.

Another break was a trip to Peru for a conference of Latin American Catholic editors in 1971. There was a large Spanish contingent led by Joaquin Ruiz Jiminez whom I had known from his undergraduate days before the war. Since then he had served in General Franco's government as Minister of Education and later as Ambassador to the Holy See. After that he retired to his law practice and became merged with the liberal – and powerless – opposition. He ran an *avant-garde* Catholic monthly which qualified him for the trip.

Where the conference funds came from I had no idea, but our congress was royally entertained. Flying into Lima gave me my first sight of a Latin American shanty-town: acres of mud-coloured huts alongside the shining city. We visited the president in his palace, a pudgy little general who listened politely to an eloquent discourse by Joaquin on justice and peace and human rights – matters quite foreign to the president – who responded with a few words and a generous supply of wine. The changing of the guard was an impressive sight with its intricate movements in slow goose-steps which I saw repeated years later in the Kremlin: these ballet steps must be very painful to the performers. Congresses of this kind are important mainly for their leisure moments when friendships and new ideas sprout up so easily.

The little group of journalists broke up. Some of us went by way of an ancient aircraft and a mountain railway to Machu Picchu, a city-fortress built of huge blocks of stone on a mountain-top, an everlasting monument to the Incas and their pagan civilisation, demolished by the Spaniards.

I reflected that, ironically, after centuries the ancient paganism has been superseded by the modern paganism so obvious in cities such as the Colombian capital Bogota, La Paz in Bolivia and Caracas, the capital of Venezuela, where I went later. But their redemption is perhaps a little nearer than they know. There were many signs of Catholic vitality in Bogota, especially among those connected with the famous Medellin conference of Catholic bishops, most of whose initiatives have given the title-deeds to liberation theology. In Caracas I gave a talk to students of the Jesuit university and saw springs of hope in that city of gross luxury and abject poverty.

Meeting again with Joaquim Ruiz Jimenez and his Spanish colleagues enabled me to hear news of friends, family and contacts. I had, of course, been back to Spain many times since the war and on one such occasion planned to meet Mabél at Madrid airport. We were meant to visit the family home once more; Gregorio Marañon had died by that time (1968), but his indomitable widow kept the house going without visiting it, leaving the family to maintain its tradition as a haven open to the world.

Mabél met me at the airport. 'We must go straight to Toledo; we have a guest for the night.'

'Who?'

'De Gaulle.'

She explained that the family had been asked by the French ambassador if the General could be put up for the night, with Madame de Gaulle and an aide, because for some reason the embassy was inconvenient. He was on a private visit calling briefly on General Franco (not far off in his country residence) and particularly to see Toledo cathedral – but not the Alcazar, that historic military establishment.

Carmen, my sister-in-law, had acquired a seven-foot bed and sent her cook and butler plus supplies of food and wine. The stage was set. The great man had all the air of a solicitous grand-parent, as did his wife. He was somewhat surprised and not entirely pleased to confront *un anglais* in these particular surroundings, but was courtesy itself. In answer to his enquiry I told him that I was editor of *The Tablet*. 'Le Tablet? *O la la!!* Le Tablet *a été très méchant avec moi*', he exclaimed in a joking fashion. He gave no explanation but I think he must have been referring to my predecessor's strong disapproval of his blocking tactics towards British approaches to the European Community.

To be so close to one who had been a protagonist in world events, in Europe's greatest crisis and France's greatest hour, was an awesome experience, all the more so for De Gaulle's humanity and humility. He and his wife simply joined the family for a few hours: time and great events were swallowed up in an atmosphere of spontaneous friendship.

The last major event while I was editor was the Argentine invasion of the Falklands in 1982. I was staying in our second home – a house in Andalusia by the sea – when the news came in a telephone call from my youngest son, Jimmy, the *Financial Times* correspondent in Buenos Aires at the time. Jimmy was a very keen observer and had spotted all the signs of trouble many weeks beforehand. Our own intelligence service and the Foreign Office were apparently taken by surprise. Another war was an

*Douglas Woodruff, my
predecessor as editor of*
The Tablet *(1936–67)*

*After-dinner conversation
with Stanley Morison (c.
1960), on board the S.S.*
Queen Elizabeth

*Our house in Mazagon,
Spain; (below) the longest
holiday, 1992*

LAS
COLUMNAS

appalling prospect. This particular one seemed to me within the scope of the United Nations and capable of a diplomatic solution. I held the view and maintained it in the paper until the shooting started. There was no other policy appropriate to *The Tablet*. It did not prevent me, of course, from hoping for speedy victory once my country was committed to battle.

Meanwhile preparations were well advanced for the first-ever papal visit to Britain. Suddenly it looked as if it could not happen. Cardinal Hume, who had asked me to stay on as editor till after the papal visit, now told me that the Vatican view was that the Pope could not visit a country at war with another lest he be accused of taking sides. I saw the dilemma and suggested a way out: put it to the Pope that he visit Argentina immediately after his visit to Britain. The proposal was put and accepted and acted upon, enormously to the Pope's credit. He was able to preach peace in both countries within a few days of each other.

It was the morning of a press day at *The Tablet* (28 October 1974) with its inevitable bustle and tension when a telephone call came to me to tell me that David Jones had died in his sleep. News of this kind never has its full impact at the time. Death may be sudden but, like a stone dropped into a pond, the ripples reach the fringe of one's surrounding consciousness in succession, over a long time. So I did my job and wrote a piece just in time for the printer.

I had seen David only a few days earlier, as well as he had ever been for some years. Now was the ending of a friendship going back even to the time when he was at Ditchling in Eric Gill's little community of craftsmen and artists, close on fifty years ago. Innumerable articles and several books have now been written about his life and work. But it comes to me now to write something more personal, in the form of a letter. We had exchanged very few in his lifetime as we were so often together. (The letters he wrote to me in Madrid have been published in *Dai*

Greatcoat.) One, written now, eighteen years after his death, is just a *reprise* of some themes that come to mind.

Dear David
Soon after you began your constant visits to the house in Chelsea which I shared with my doctor brother, you became an anchor-man of our regular Saturday lunches and our not-infrequent parties. The first were serious and almost Socratic, often lasting late into the evening; the second were a rich mixture from the fringes of high bohemia. I can see you now, crouched on the corner of a divan with two or three graceful girls draped round you in earnest discussion. In a strange way you seemed to set the tone of the party. There was something magnetic about you: the small unkempt, unknown painter from Brockley – from outer space as far as most people in the room were concerned.

Trench language and the realism that lay behind it coloured your talk. It seemed to put you at ease with everyone, though there was no obvious common bond. I noticed the same in a private hotel where you took refuge for a time – the Fort in Sidmouth. Having made a weekend dash from London in my Wolsely Hornet, I would find you chatting to elderly ladies and retired colonels before or after dinner. There would be breaks, of course: 'Let's go for a wet,' you would whisper, and we were off to the local for a pint.

Our jaunts together were memorable. Once we were told by a knowing friend that there was an Inn at Hartland Point which might be guaranteed not to have the slightest hint of the commercialised Christmas from which were were in flight. It was a lovely spot indeed but we came down to dinner to find two paper hats on our dinner table. Once we went to the great Carthusian monastery at Parkminster in Sussex for a couple of days. But 24 hours sufficed to convince us that the great contemplative powerhouse was not for us, minnows among deep-sea fish.

Caldey was different – an island off the Welsh coast owned by the monastery of French Trappists, one of the most austere of contemplative orders. With Harman Grisewood we hired a cottage by the sea, run by a bountiful Welsh woman who mothered us for a couple of weeks. You painted all day; Harman and I had a lot of editorial work to do but also explored little islands nearby, uninhabited and cut off at high tide. Once we waded back from one of them through a race-tide that threatened to sweep us away. You showed a restrained relief when we staggered ashore from the swirling waist-high waters.

A very different jaunt was our trip to Cairo, to stay in eastern luxury with Ralph and Manya Harari. To get you equipped and actually aboard the P&O boat in London dock was a long haul; you were in the depth of a nervous depression and everything was frightening. But we sailed and immediately you found immense relief in the cabin-comfort and the positive and immediate devotion of your Goanese steward. By the time we reached Gibraltar you had been often out on deck and were greeting other passengers, but the idea of boarding a lighter with the rest of them to visit Gib was too much for you. When the last of the lighters had left there were a few dinghies bobbing about and calling for custom. 'Come on, let's go', you suddenly said, so off we went at much greater discomfort and expense than all the other passengers. But you had made a leap into reality – away from the 'heebie-jeebies' and 'Rosie' as I used to call your neurotic 'come-overs'. Your depression had quite disappeared by the time we got to Cairo and I was happy to leave you in the hands of the Hararis, in palatial peace.

That was in 1934. It was the last of our outings together. You went on to Jerusalem where Eric Gill was working on a monument. I remember your telling me that one day you saw him from the window of your hotel coming down the street – stop by a leprous beggar squatting in the gutter, drop a coin into his bowl and kiss him, thinking himself unobserved. That seems to me to put paid to critics of his morals.

I came back by a lovely little ship to Venice and then home by train. Today it could all have been done by air – and how much we would have missed! It is better to travel hopefully than to arrive; but nowadays one just arrives. You were in good shape after Cairo and Jerusalem: painting and writing as never before. You visited many friends and came like a homing pigeon to my flat in Glebe Place from time to time. They were busy years for me; the publishing business was all-absorbing, but I was in something of a turmoil in my human affections. You took some of the frenzy out of them, having fore-suffered so much. You came to know all the girls that I knew. As the odds and the tensions narrowed to two, and then one, you were at ease, in a happy relationship with all, whereas mine was disjointed and sometimes desperate.

I have come to think that our happiest times were in those darkest years just before the war. They were dark indeed. Munich, of course, proved to be an illusory hope, but the vociferous opponents of that settlement filled us with despair. There were those who were looking forward in every sense to war: bridling, truculent, offensive, arrogant and in deadly earnest. Churchill was their prophet. They took delight in his defiance of all diplomatic endeavour to avert the catastrophe. I had many dissident German Catholic friends, exiles all. We would meet regularly but with litte comfort beyond the belief that Europe would not commit suicide. But it did.

There was the realism of politics, inexorably working towards its own extinction. There was also a realism in our own consciences, making for an independence of spirit, born of a dependence on God. That was the ultimate lesson of those years, bringing freedom from fear. Such a growth was like that of plants, best brought up in the dark. Call them hyacinth days. We were curiously happy when everything exploded.

It began, of course, with the 'phoney war' when nothing happened and it was at that time that I took off for Spain, supposedly for a couple of weeks. But I did not get leave to arrange my affairs for several months. I remember coming back to the flat unannounced and finding you and the friends that I had left you with still there, as if time had stood still. It was great joke but it couldn't last. We both went to our appointed places and different existences. I put all my books and furniture into a store which was later bombed to cinders.

After the war I came into a different world. I had a wife, a home and also a baby on the way. You went to live in a boarding-house in Harrow, admirably conducted by an ex-housemaster of the school. It was your kind of place in many ways and all your friends were happy about it. But it had to come to an end and you moved to a private hotel which, you said, was rather like a Turkish brothel. How did you know? Anyway, they were kind there and took in all your books and endless paraphernalia.

Then came a mild heart attack; then hospital; then your last move to a peaceful nursing-home run by nuns called Calvary Nursing Home. With such a name it didn't seem to promise what most you needed. But it turned out to be a lovely place, high up on a Harrow hill overlooking London – beyond the wilderness of its large garden. The nuns were as good and kind as could be and you took their ministrations with grace and patience – even those awful meals on trays, brought in with such relentless regularity. My visits were at weekend and in the evening mostly and my Saab would sweep up the drive into this other dimension of yours. What kept us going was what you would call a 'meandering conversation' which had been going on for years.

You had no fear of death; you had none in two world wars in quite different circumstances; you would have hated all the apparatus of 'intensive care'. You left behind great and permanent achievements both in paint and writing. And you had royal recognition which, to you, had a sacramental quality. Companion of Honour is a gift of the Sovereign and when you were offered it you regretfully refused it on the grounds that a visit to Buckingham Palace was beyond your strength. It was rapidly explained that there was no difficulty and an equerry arrived with the emblem in due course, with a letter solicitous about your health. I remember how, for the earlier honour of the CBE, you had in fact been to the Palace (this was in 1955). The Queen asked you what you did. You answered simply, 'I paint pictures and your mother has quite a collection of them.'

The Church, which you always loved like an occasionally tiresome mother, offered a great funeral Mass in Westminster Cathedral. For the last time I was with the concourse of your friends. Many did not know each other: you were a private person to so many. Their own memories will die with them one by one but what will survive is the only thing you really cared for – and for which you sacrificed everything – your art. Some will come to learn of the passion and humility behind its achiever; for myself, I doubt if any other mortal soul has been such a counsellor, such a kind comrade.

I left the paper to John Wilkins who had been my assistant editor in the early years of my term. He had spent a profitable period at the BBC in the meantime and gained invaluable experience. He came back to the paper with new enthusiasm and energy and, without departing from my general lines, he has increased the paper's scope, and brought in new talent. I left *The Tablet* with no regrets and great confidence in its future. Today the list of subscribers is more than double what it was when I took over from Douglas Woodruff.

The Tablet Trust, established in May 1976 and now the cornerstone of the publishing company, was born of two convictions which came to me after a couple of years in the editor's chair. First, that a paper with *The Tablet*'s special responsibility and representative character must have the financial standing and stability to match. Secondly, that the editor, while his independence must be totally assured, should be chosen and implicitly supported by a responsible group of Catholics, rather than having to confront the world on his own, so to speak (Douglas Woodruff and I were virtually self-chosen!).

There had been times when I had felt myself, quite unwarrantably as it turned out, to be without support. When I began to seek out possible trustees I was overjoyed at the response. My first approach was to the Duke of Norfolk; his agreement was immediate and enthusiastic. I recognised that he was not only a friend but a leader for laymen like his great forebear, that duke to whom Newman had addressed his famous letter on conscience and on other matters of doctrine – although of course there are some marked differences between my lively, direct and downright major-general and the grave and bearded Victorian gentleman who had been so wise in critical times for the Church in England in Victorian times.

I went on to see Sir John Hunt, at that time the Cabinet Secretary. He readily accepted my invitation, having already shown keen and practical interest in the paper. (Later as Lord Hunt of Tanworth he succeeded me as chairman of *The Tablet* board of directors when I retired from the scene.) I went on to recruit Charles Curran (RIP) who was director general of the BBC, and William Rees-Mogg, at the time editor of *The Times*. Both gave their backing. The world might well have rubbed its eyes to see Roman Catholics in such Establishment positions.

In the world of commerce and finance Lord Forte gave not only his name but considerable financial help. It turned out that the chairman of Kleinwort Benson, Gerald Thompson, was a regular reader and he joined not only the trustees but my board. One of my oldest and most faithful supporters, Don Frank Doria-Pamphilj, wrote an acceptance from Rome, and that colourful tycoon Tony O'Reilly (the head of Heinz of baked-beans fame) wrote from Pittsburgh calling me the gentlest arm-twister he had ever met. In a quiet corner of Pratt's, Graham Greene joined up, and so it went on.

This list is too long to follow right through. We are today twenty-five trustees, allowing for deaths and newcomers. Rather more than half that number meet for business once or twice a year at my club – the Garrick – and finish off the evening by dining there. We have one guest at a time; Cardinal Hume and Archbishop Runcie were among the first, with excellent 'off the record' talk.

Looking back on so many difficult years it seemed to me that, very late in the day, with the Trust *The Tablet* had acquired a new dimension.

13

Roman Interludes

Not in extended time, but in depth Rome has affected my being more than all other cities. I have been there off and on since my teenage years and have always come away with some indefinable enrichment. To me it is a city beyond compare. Others may better it with the art of a particular epoch. The broad sweep of Rome covers all epochs. It could so well be just a museum city, so evocative, so intriguing at every glance, so instructive. But it is alive with a contagious vitality. Every corner teaches history, and its people live it.

The narrow noisy and twisting streets of medieval and renaissance Rome so often end in a piazza with fountains playing. The *mis-en-scène* is of Renaissance palaces and baroque churches, market-places full of colour and movement, a great jungle of buildings, from bordellos to basilicas, confronting the stark grey ruins of Imperial Rome's temples, triumphal arches and the grim, ghost-ridden Colosseum.

I see it in snapshots of incidents, it defies a static, panoramic view. My first journey to Rome, in October 1926 when I was twenty, was *en route* to Assisi where there were to be great celebrations to honour the sixth centenary of St Francis. The little town – one of the loveliest in Europe – was packed with pilgrims. It was useless to look for a lodging for the night. I found a rounded ditch on the outskirts, on a hillside facing the setting sun. I was travelling rough with a small rucksack. With this for a pillow and some old newspapers for cover, I slept blissfully under the stars.

At sunrise I went to a fountain where peasants were sluicing their sleepy faces and did likewise. At that moment the portentous figure of Cardinal Merry del Val came down the street with his retinue. (He was the papal legate for this great occasion.) As he scattered blessings like invisible confetti over the crowded pavement I could not resist jumping up and telling him that I was at Stonyhurst with his nephews Alfonso and Pablo. He stopped, seemingly dumbfounded by my uncouth appearance. Then, 'Splendid,' he said, 'you must come and serve my Mass.' The retinue fell back and we walked together to the cathedral where I covered my rough clothes with a cassock and was transformed into an acolyte, well-trained for the function from my schooldays. It was my first touch of Rome with its splendours and its surprises, and its humanity.

There was something of all these elements on my next visit. Harman Grisewood telephoned me from the BBC, where he was one of the chief announcers, to ask whether I would go with him immediately to Rome to cover the burial of Pope Pius XI. 'You'll be able to pull strings for me – I know nobody there. The BBC will pay all expenses.' It was an irresistible invitation. I had only one string to pull but a very effective one: a raffish Italian prince of Italo-American patronage, whom I happened to know, was in charge of Italian-English relations at Radio Nazionale. He was more than helpful. In due course Harman found himself in St Peter's at a dizzy height in the cupola, fully equipped with all the apparatus required in those days for outside broadcasting, thanks to my friend, Prince William Rospigliosi. For myself, I had no magic pass for a close-up view of the ceremonies – except bluff. I put on white tie and tails and mingled with the diplomatic corps, passing in stately procession through the huge bronze doors of the Vatican.

We were shepherded to a privileged place next to the high altar, overlooking the entrance to the crypt and St Peter's tomb. A temporary derrick, of medieval design with rope and pulley, was used to lower the heavy ornate coffin into the depths. At the end of the Solemn Requiem the coffin was hoisted from the ground and for a moment hung dangling over the descent to the crypt. The pulleys creaked, the coffin swung in mid-air, slowly descending. 'If only those ropes would break!' came a fervent prayer in English at my elbow. I turned and beheld no less a personage than Tom Driberg, a gossip columnist on the *Daily Express*. He was dressed as I was and went whiter than his shirt-front at my reproving '*Shoosh.*' (Driberg was a Communist, a notorious pederast, later to be an MP and elevated to the Lords by Mr Harold Wilson.) 'What on earth are *you* doing here?' we asked each other. All reverentially dispersed when the coffin had come to rest.

Later I was closeted with Harman and the prince in the bowels of Radio Nazionale. International broadcasting was not so easy in those days; both men were on tenterhooks, as the telephone connection to London for Harman's final broadcast fluctuated. The lights flickered and, unexpectedly, the red light came on, interrupting the prince's frantic instructions. '*Bugger*,' said he and the word went out to the world. Harman proceeded with his report of the historic proceedings. Our duty done we went happily home after a celebratory dinner with Roy Campbell who was living in Rome at the time. He was off alcohol after a pilgrimage to Fatima but the *aqua minerale* worked on him like champagne. It was a fine celebration. We had buried the indomitable hammer of Communists and Nazis, the tough Milanese mountaineer, Achille Ratti, Pope Pius XI.

My first Roman visit after the war was to his successor Eugenio Pacelli, Pius XII, in private audience with my wife. The new Pope was a Roman aristocrat, full of grace, sacred and profane. 'You could only be a Spaniard,' he said to Mabél, 'carrying your mantilla as you do.' Courtesy visits to *il Papa* never rise above social banalities. They were not expected to raise any matter of importance. All the same they show a typical trait of *Romanitá*: to be both worldly and reverential at the same time. The present Pope is too busy for private audiences: he deals with people in groups with a brief handshake and a word or two; the ceremony is known as *bacci di mano*.

As publisher to the Holy See I had two more audiences with Pius XII and two with Paul VI: matters of custom and convenience, but both popes were scholars and book-lovers and handled the books that I brought as would any other bibliophile, forgetting protocol, talking easily about them, commenting on the layout. One felt that one was providing a brief respite from the endless preoccupations and besetting problems of their unique governance.

There are two men in Rome with spiritual power only exceeded by that of the Pope: the General of the Jesuits, generally known as the Black Pope, and the head of the now worldwide organisation, Opus Dei. They are mostly inaccessible in their respective headquarters. The influence of both spreads throughout the world, through universities, schools, missions and groups dedicated to specialised spiritual tasks. The Jesuit order is by far the greater of the two and goes back 450 years; Opus Dei is in its sixties.

In one visit to Rome my wife and I were received by the Jesuit General. Fr Arrupe was a Basque with the lineaments of Ignatius Loyola, another Basque and founder of the Jesuits. He had narrowly escaped the effects of the atomic bomb on Hiroshima where he happened to be. He was a polyglot and had travelled throughout the world. He was a man of courtesy and charm with a hint of holiness.

The founder and head of Opus Dei was also a Spaniard, coming from Aragon. The physical and mental contrast with Fr Arrupe was total. Mgr Escrivá de Balaguer was rotund, loquacious, emotional; Fr Arrupe was his opposite in every particular. I was highly privileged to know them both through their quite different connections with my father-in-law, Dr Marañon. Fr Arrupe had begun life as a medical student who – like all his contemporaries – held Marañon in reverence. Mgr Escriva's connection with Don Gregorio was indeed far-fetched. At the outbreak of the Spanish Civil War, when Communist death squads roamed Madrid, he had taken refuge in a lunatic asylum. When the *milicianos*, so-called, came to the place to check up on the inmates, they asked this apparent lunatic who he was. Mgr Escriva told me that instinctively and without forethought he said he was Dr Marañon. His insanity was thus obvious and they left him alone.

The Jesuit headquarters are in the shadow of the Vatican, an austere anonymous building without ornament of any kind. Here the General directs his far-flung empire with the help of advisers (*socii*) from every country of the world. He received my wife and me with courteous charm in his sparsely furnished study. It was an awesome encounter in the way that charity can be awesome.

Mgr Escriva's headquarters are in the middle of Rome. He sat in an ornate office backed by a six-foot portrait of himself in the robes of a knight of one of the military orders. He had reclaimed a title of nobility which had been lost in times past and was duly granted arms and the title of marquis. We were more than once interrupted by messengers who dropped on one knee to deliver their missives (I suspect he had a buzzer under the desk to summon them). He addressed us as he would at a public meeting: exhorting and denouncing and appealing by turns, with lots of laughter thrown in. I came away with more questions than answers in my mind.

Opus Dei is based on a little book of maxims called *The Way* which has been translated into every language. The secular movement (priests are a small minority) has captured some first-class brains and sterling characters. Its followers, who are often high in their profession, have *The Way* for their bible. It was once described to me by a well-known German theologian as 'spiritual boy-scoutism'. Yet there are achievements of Opus Dei in many fields which are outstanding. It is integralist to the core and much favoured by Pope John Paul. The founder is already on the way to canonisation, on which matter I have serious reservations.

The generous mantle of Rome covers both Jesuits and Opus Dei not to speak of countless other religious orders and organisations, each with their special character and motivation.

This complex multiplicity of religious life in Rome seems to minister to every imaginable human need. There is nothing monolithic about it. I was not surprised to see the general of the Order of Preachers – the Dominicans – and Mother Teresa in the same ante-room of the papal apartments waiting for an audience. She let me kiss her hand, gently smiling. To be timeless, to be alert to every happening, to be serious, to be possessor of an inward joy – these were qualities of the Vatican which I came to appreciate more with each successive visit, without being blind to its defects.

To all this should be added an infinite resilience which was especially revealed to me at Vatican II, the Second Vatican Council (1962–65), when some 3,000 bishops from all parts of the world, with their respective advisers and chaplains, descended on the Vatican. They lived in their national seminaries and colleges to emerge in busloads, bound for St Peter's: black bishops, yellow bishops, Hispanic bishops, Nordic bishops; in a jolly way they would wave to passers-by and then disappear. There was ever a festive air about the Council. Even in the solemn sessions in St Peter's a bishop could slip away to the underground Bar-Jonah, as it was called, for an *espresso* and a smoke. I was often a welcomed intruder there. The bishops seemed to be in holiday mood despite the long sessions, the heavy paperwork and the demands of various committees.

I was only able to visit Rome three times while the Council was in progress, but the intervals gave a chance to observe its corporate growth, how the Council gradually assumed a personality and authority of its own. When it ended it had come to conclusions by no means acceptable to more conservative Vatican minds and had in fact brought about changes in the Church with results still emerging or still being blocked. At one stage I stayed with my old friend the Spanish Ambassador to the Holy See, Antonio Garrigues, in the vast Palazzo di Spagna where centuries ago 600 Spanish troops had been quartered for its protection. The ambassador would occasionally offer a great luncheon to the members of a foreign hierarchy. This gave me a unique opportunity for personal contacts with bishops from all over the world, as well as other groups such as the Taizé community. By contrast the ambassador would use his smaller dining-room for informal gatherings and I was free to invite leading theologians, who would otherwise have been outside his orbit. Here we kindled our common interest in theological development in the friendliest atmosphere. Dr Delahaye of Louvain, the Dutch Dominican Père Schillebeeckx, the Swiss professor from Tübingen Hans Küng, our own Bishop Butler, the French Jesuit Henri de Lubac were among the guests whom I still remember. De Lubac had been silenced for his advanced theological views before the Council, but was given the significant honour of concelebrating with the Pope in the final High Mass. He died a cardinal.

It has often been said that the spirit of Cardinal Newman presided over the Council. Its practical application was largely in the capable hands of the Belgian Cardinal Suenens. It made me realise that the liberal spirit is as much a mark of the Roman Church as is its authoritarian structure, exemplified supremely in the Curia. This is the governing body of the Church under the Pope, with its various 'congregations' ruling over all aspects of doctrine and discipline. Liberty and authority are indeed necessary to each other.

The Curia is normally inaccessible to the layman but I made two penetrations into its fortress which revealed its hidden humanity. Burns & Oates published the official Roman texts of various liturgical rites. One of them dealt with the reception of Christian converts. It struck me that the new form about to be promulgated was so worded as to cause unnecessary offence, belittling as it did the convert's previous spiritual adherence and experience. I took the text in proof form to one of the under-secretaries of state, a curial archbishop and an old acquaintance. He was taken by surprise. 'Dear me', he said in Americanised English, 'that won't do. Leave it to me', and he took up his telephone to talk to the Congregation of Rites. After a long animated conversation in Italian which I could not follow the archbishop turned to me with a smile; 'All's well, we will knock out the passage.' So it happened.

The other occasion concerned a personal problem. I was deeply worried about a certain matrimonial case which was likely to drag on indefinitely in the Congregation of the Sacraments. An Anglican marriage had been dissolved by the English court and likewise by the Roman ecclesiastical court in London. It was an open-shut case, but I had been told in London that the final decision, depending on the Pope's signature, might be delayed for six months or more. Meanwhile the case constituted an impediment to a true marriage which meant life itself to the young couple concerned. I decided to go to Rome: 'Give me six days,' I said to the head of the London ecclesiastical court.

I went again to stay with the Spanish Ambassador to the Holy See and explained the case. He gave me an introduction to the Prefect of the Congregation of the Sacraments, asking for me to be given an urgent interview on a personal matter. Diplomatic correspondence with the Curia is on a heavy parchment-like paper and typed in capitals far beyond the scope of an ordinary typewriter, at least such was the case with this missive. It vouched for my *bona-fides* and other personal qualities in terms embarrassing to me without reference to the reason for the visit. It worked. The Cardinal-Prefect would see me immediately. I found a charming old gentleman in his secluded residence of modest grandeur. He had been for many years a nuncio in Latin America and his Spanish was perfect, making it easy for me to speak *'de hombre a hombre'*, as I said. I spoke from the heart and after a patient listening he responded. 'All will be well. Leave it to me.' I gave the number of a file for reference which London had given me. He then showed me little art treasures he had collected in his time as nuncio and we parted with an embrace in the Spanish fashion.

Two days later a secretary of the Curia happened to be lunching at the embassy. 'What have you done to the Congregation? It's in a commotion.' The papers came through in two days, well within my limit. Back in London my canon lawyer chuckled with delight. 'You've caused a revolution.' I felt for so many other people in similar cases who were, in all likelihood, not possessed of my privileges, but I was assured that procedures in future would be speeded up.

Another visit to the Curia was to pay my respects to Cardinal Tisserant, Prefect of the Sacred College, *ex officio* in charge of the Church when the Holy See became vacant through death. This was before the promulgation of *Humanae Vitae* but after the conclusions of the papal Commission had become known. I tried to steer the conversation in that direction, hoping for an opinion. The cardinal gave me the impression of never having heard of the Commission and spent much time showing me his albums where he had stuck the visiting cards of innumerable disting-uished visitors – like a schoolboy with his stamp collection.

I had another *palazzo* as a frequent port of call, that of the Doria-Pamphilj family, a vast building facing on the Piazza Venezia where Mussolini used to orate from a balcony. The Prince Doria of the time would close all his shutters whenever *il Duce* appeared. He went into hiding in the popular *barrio* of Trastevere when the Germans arrived. The humble people there loved him and hid him. When the Allies took over he was made Mayor of Rome. His wife was Scottish and their only daughter married an RNVR officer while she was doing hospital work in Brindisi after Italy had left the war. It is a long romantic story on its own which still continues. As far as I was concerned, Frank Pogson and his wife Orietta were wonderful friends. They substantially backed *The Tablet* in its difficult transition period when I took over. Their unobtrusive generosity in many Catholic causes, their hospitality towards the less official side in Catholic affairs was sure-footed. Some cardinals and the 'black' Roman aristocracy might disapprove, but the Dorias were a law unto themselves – as the family had been for centuries.

The Abbey of Sant' Anselmo stands on the Aventine hill,

tenuously connected to the bustling centre of the city by a white ribbon of winding road. It is in Rome but not of it. I stayed there on my last visit to Rome at the invitation of the prior, my nephew and godson, now headmaster of Ampleforth. Sant' Anselmo is the secretariat and study house for the Benedictines from all parts of the world. There are no 'headquarters' of the order, for all abbeys are autonomous. Their self-sufficient communities, so much a feature of Catholic life, give variety to the Church and stimulus to their members.

The abbey was a good place for saying goodbye to the city. I had not dropped a coin in the Trevi fountain to ensure my return, as pilgrims do. Maybe I shall never go back, but Rome constantly returns to me: an inescapable presence to the mind. The eye, too, has its own memory. I conjure up the Sistine Chapel as easily as any *trattoria* in Trastevere, great ceremonies at St Peter's as well as the dark and secret corridors of the Catacombs, where my Jesuit brother once said Mass for me and my wife, like a *revenant* from the first century. Taken it all in all, Rome is indelibly human and indelibly sacred: thus it has the marks of the Incarnation.

14

Back to the Beginning

To wake up one morning a private person was a delectable experience. After fifteen years with *The Tablet* my time was my own and the only question was how to spend it. For years past I had been a desultory 'Sunday painter'. I decided to take a refresher course conducted by a Royal Academician at a summer school on the Welsh border. Mabél and I set off without more ado, to settle in a little inn near my master's summer studio. He was an excellent teacher, leading by example. I came fresh to the long-neglected lessons of my eyes. Now they discovered new tones in the landscape, unsuspected planes and colours, the relationship of trees with their shadows, fields like a plaid shawl. Nothing matters, nobody is remembered in this time of loving regard. It is akin to religious contemplation, an unspoken prayer of praise.

Soon after this idyllic existence some family action was needed. We decided to sell the big flat by Westminster Cathedral as we were now on our own. After much searching all over south-west London we came back almost to where we had started. The flat in Buckingham Gate is a small replica of what we left and even nearer the heart of London: a short walk takes us to St James's Park; all the surroundings were familiar, there was no traumatic change.

We decided to visit two of our boys across the Atlantic: David, then a merchant banker in New York, and Jimmy, the *Financial Times* man in Buenos Aires. Any city is what one makes it. New York was for me no longer a busy publisher's marketplace but a new scene. We stayed with David and his sparkling Italian wife, Carola, in an apartment in the eighties off Lexington Avenue, a quiet residential and professional area, as an estate agent would put it, but for us a starting point for the patchwork of contrasting cultures that make up the city. The subway which links them together is hectic, noisy and sinister, but at street level there is an atmosphere of rough, anonymous, jostling friendliness, of a people dwarfed by serene sky-scrapers and controlled at every corner by traffic lights and ubiquitous cops. Humanity is not cowed but asserts itself under these pressures. Even the foul manners of the taxi-drivers are a sort of unquestioning acceptance of fellow citizens.

The contrast with Washington where we went next is extreme. In its wide and seemingly endless avenues nobody moves except on wheels. We were welcomed by Archie and 'Lucky' Roosevelt whom we had known in Madrid at the United States Embassy. By now Lucky, a dark-eyed sprite from the Lebanon, was head of protocol at the White House. Archie was now revealed to us as a high executive in the CIA, the diplomatic gloves were off, but he was still his chubby charming quizzical self. He died, still young, not long after our reunion.

Washington had other memories. It must have been in 1935 that I was there principally to see Paul Claudel who was French ambassador at the time. I had just published *The Satin Slipper*, a translation of *Le Soulier de Satin*, possibly his greatest poetic drama. He had been passed over for election to the *Académie Française* – a mean gesture which would have horrified its founder, Cardinal Richelieu. At his overflowing luncheon table I conveyed my dismay. His reaction was memorable: 'Don't be worried, *cher ami*; the Academy is like a *bordel*, its delights may be immediate but they do not last.' He spoke with a conviction which, I conjectured, was born of experience. What had indeed lasted, surmounting every trial, was his profound faith, his mystical realism and his poetic genius.

Finally we came to rest in the quiet heartland of America, at

Springfield, Illinois. Hugh and Jane Garvey were old friends from publishing days, so we could relax in Lincoln's birthplace. I devoured his biography and this colossus of a man grew in my imagination. In common with every other schoolboy and undergraduate, I had hardly heard of him, bogged down as we all were in the sterile terrain of our own deplorable Tudors.

After Christmas it was Jimmy's turn and we planned to visit him in Buenos Aires. He had been the correspondent for the *Financial Times* all through the Falklands war, but his perfect Spanish and his mother's maiden name, Marañon, had been a safeguard. (He tells the whole dramatic story in *The Land which lost its Heroes* (1987), which won a Somerset Maugham prize.) He had arranged the trip to perfection. It involved picking up a visa in the Argentine consulate in Rio – an achievement of his when Britain had no diplomatic relations with Argentina. An obliging Foreign Minister had apparently bent the rules. Rio is pandemonium and scarcely veiled violence: the violence of the bag snatchers and muggers on the waterfront, the violence of luxury hotels vaunting it over slums – the *favellas* – which in their abject ghastliness reminded me of Calcutta, except the Brazilian vitality has its own tempo. There were by-ways of peace and beauty shown to us by Jimmy's *Financial Times* colleague. Jimmy himself has described in his book *Across the Silver River* (1989) one slum area which has been redeemed by a Jesuit priest, creating a community at peace with itself.

We flew on to the Argentine frontier at Iguaçu, meeting Jimmy there and crossing a river to a different world. The first encounter was with gigantic waterfalls. Nature was here rampant and recklessly spendthrift: it was an amber torrent and the boom, crash and sparkle of the waters seemed to sing of some aboriginal catastrophe of nature long before the coming of mankind.

We moved on through woods and plains to a territory still called *Misiones*, the missions. The sad story goes back to the seventeenth century and tells of a human achievement inspired by divine grace which has few parallels in human history and yet is almost unknown. In its way it is more mysterious and awe-inspiring than any phenomenon of wild nature, nature never has the note of tragedy, which only exists among human beings. In 1608 a handful of Spanish Jesuit priests was sent from Paraguay to evangelise the Indian aborigines in the far west. Here a tribe, the Guarani, singularly gifted in peaceful pursuits, open to the world of the spirit, was being ruthlessly raided by slave-traders from Sao Paolo in Brazil and being sold into slavery.

The first act of the missionaries was to transport them in canoes down the River Paraná out of harm's way. By 1631, slavers had wrenched 60,000 Indians from their homeland but many thousands were saved and settled in great enclosures, each a microcosm of civilisation. They aroused the jealousy and suspicion of their overlords thousands of miles away in Spain. King Charles III decreed expulsion of the Jesuits from Spain and all Spanish possessions. An ideal – perhaps the only example of 'liberation theology' to have existed in history – was shattered. Its monument is in the gaunt walls in rose-red and yellow stone, the columns and the broken arches and carvings: a shattered sanctuary like a giant skeleton prostrate in an open grave, stretching as far as the eye can see.

Finally we reached Buenos Aires – a hint of Paris with London suburbs. In one of them Jimmy and 'Kidge' – my only English daughter-in-law – had their home; a neat little house with a garden back and front. Happily for all of us the back garden was taken up by a swimming pool. The long hot summer was not yet over. An electric train at the end of our leafy road rattled into the capital every hour.

Jimmy knew every corner of the capital: from the Jockey Club, which is all London clubs rolled into one, to the *tabernas* by the Bocca, the great port. By its position and its grandeur the British Embassy betokened the British influence in the Argentina of earlier generations – an influence which has now totally disappeared. Officially the embassy itself no longer existed, its affairs were in the hands of the Swiss. The British representative remained incognito and we dined with him and his wife, having been discreetly admitted by the back door. Other guests were British owners of *haciendas* and other enterprises who seemed to have been left undisturbed by the Falklands war. Indeed, to them it seemed to be a distant and local skirmish. Our host, David Joy, had seen it through with all its dangers of failure so gallantly overcome and was waiting for happier days.

There was something nostalgic about that dinner in that place, a sense of a past that could not be recaptured, when *la palabra inglesa* was as good a surety as a signed cheque and the marks of England were everywhere; even the buffers in the station carried 'Made in England' in bold letters. Leaving Argentina was like leaving the house of someone's broken marriage. The traces of a long and happy bond were now only just discernible.

Our next objective, which I had not originally envisaged, was Chile, and we, with Jimmy and 'Kidge', went to Mendoza and from there boarded a trans-Andean bus which wound its way to the frontier on the snow-line between giant peaks. When I saw the Chilean flag at the frontier I realised that my feeling for the country was visceral, nothing to do with sentiment or memory. I had left Chile as an infant but it had evidently infected me in the womb, as might a mother's drugs or drink. Here I was coming back with a sense of recognition, as happens sometimes with a poem never seen before. In the stiff breeze the flag was flying flat against a dark blue sky. Formalities at the frontier were perfunctory. We drank Chilean wine, of the best in the world. My blood tingled to hear the soft accentuated language as I had heard it in boyhood in our English home.

The warm air strengthened as we began our long descent. I came into a country which was effectively a family gathering, cousinship spread like ground-cover. We came among radiant people who took us to their hearts. My own contemporaries – first cousins – were, of course, very old: among them were two delightful gentlemen twins of my age, but looking much older and more benign than I ever felt. The girls of the younger generation were alight with vitality. One was married to a lawyer who was also the foreign minister at the time. He was not typical of the military dictatorship and I heard without surprise of his resignation after we had left. He appeared in his official car to take us back to the capital from a family gathering. Its only unusual feature was a Kalashnikov rifle beside the driver's seat, a hint that all was not normal. The Pinochet regime was on its last legs and police roamed the streets. We saw a scuffle with some suspected miscreant who took to his heels, making for sanctuary in the church which we had just left.

Chile is the most Europeanised country in South America. The Spanish influence is still strong there. The descendants of my father's generation – Scots, Irish and English – were now part of the business community and intermarried with women with their special Chilean charm. Maybe there will be another round of eager and adventurous young men to keep up that tradition. We left behind a whole clan who had become our friends in just a couple of weeks. They gathered in one of their houses for a goodbye *fiesta* under the stars. I heard myself making a speech in my clipped Castilian and can still hear the *vivas* at our departure: *'Viva Chile! Viva Inglaterra!'*

15

Russia: Darkness before Dawn

For my 8oth birthday, our children presented us with a trip to Moscow and Leningrad (to use its pseudonym at that time). It had to be postponed for three years owing to the Chernobyl disaster and its poisoning of the atmosphere for miles around.

I had long since wanted to visit the Soviet Union. It fascinated and repelled but never seduced me. This was not the case with so many of my contemporaries, ranging from the intelligentsia to bright creatures whose knowledge of the country hardly went beyond vodka. This history of wholesale genocide, of the horrors of the labour camps and the relentless persecution of all religion was a closed book and was blandly overlooked.

Of course, by the time of our visit, Stalin's dictatorship was past history, but Communism was not yet on its deathbed. Now, the Russian Easter has been restored and we are witnesses of a new Pentecost (but a long travail lies ahead for new acts of new apostles).

The story I had to tell in *The Tablet* has not yet lost its validity; spiritual anorexia is difficult to cure. I reprint it here without amendment, as it first appeared in *The Tablet* (21 January 1989):

In the case of people and things dear to one, absence sometimes takes on a presence of its own. There are moments of special awareness when their absence is palpable. So with religion in Russia. Statisics tell us that it is there but they mock us in their measuring of the immeasureable. Something fundamental to human nature has been banished: its absence makes itself felt at every moment. This is the lasting impression of a week spent in Moscow and Leningrad on a package tour. It is admittedly subjective but so is every view, according to Aquinas: 'Whatever is received is received according to the mode of the receiver.'

Moscow is Mecca for all Soviet citizens and they come in organised battalions from all over their vast country. As a consequence the hotels are immense: we were told that ours had 6,000 beds. You are a number not a name in the register. Your key is held against your card by a supervisor on each landing.

Our hotel is next to the heart of the Communist world. As we leave it there are three closed churches facing us, in various stages of decay. In Red Square itself, under the walls of the Kremlin, stands the cathedral of St Basil with its onion-shaped cupolas newly gilded or coloured: no longer a house of prayer but a museum, as are most churches everywhere else in the land. At right angles is Lenin's squat square mausoleum. He has been dead for more than half a century but there is a would-be semblance of life in the pickled body resting as if in a siesta in the intimacy of his homely clothes.

Apart from the apparently endless queue of visitors to the shrine, the square is almost deserted. The dark stone buildings do not make room for shop windows or cafés as one might expect of a city centre. There is nowhere to sit or saunter. It is an implacable place, and when daylight dies it leaves nobody behind except the rigid guards with fixed bayonets at the closed entrance to the tomb, relieved at intervals by a goose-stepping posse.

Next day there was a visit to the Kremlin which towers over Red Square. This is the citadel and centre of power of all Russia. A vast complex of official buildings, it has few doors open to the public. Nowhere is the rejection of God more palpable. The cathedrals of St Michael, the Annunciation and the Assumption, clustered together, have been emptied of the past and their purpose and turned into museums. The icons and the sacred vessels and vestments, out of their proper places, locked in cabinets, have something of the pathos of wild animals in a zoo.

As the Intourist guides shepherd their docile flocks from one sometime sacred place to another, their chant is of weights and measures: this candelabra weighs five tons, that sculpted cathedral door 60 tons, this spire is 260 feet high, that mosaic is no less than 20 square metres ... the hungry sheep move on. The Holy of Holies is a Lenin museum. Here the prophet is portrayed from infancy. His drab clothes in their glass case are surprisingly small: the Soviet colossus was five feet six inches tall. His bare little office, from which he ruled all Russia and hoped to rule the world, is reproduced in meticulous detail – the original is in a corner of the Council of

Ministers' building beyond the reach of mere people – and for our consolation we are told that even the pencils on the desk of the replica are aligned as they were when he left them.

The guide reads out from one of Lenin's innumerable notes where he warns his colleagues against Stalin as a crafty, cruel and ambitious man, unsuitable to be general secretary of the Party. One may suppose that only a few years ago this display would have been unthinkable, remembering that Stalin was once Lenin's bed-mate in the tomb before his corpse was removed to a subordinate sepulchre.

Perhaps Zagorsk would be different: a monastery town, the seat and shrine of the Church, Russia's Canterbury, by a straight road 75 kilometres north-west of the capital. Perhaps here something had been kept alight, a little candle shining like a good deed in a naughty world.

A square above a mound, surrounded by chapels and churches of contorted or else classically simple architecture, coloured or white, fortress-like or fantastic – yet churches all the same and places of prayer. Only two were alive with the liturgy. Here peasant women with heads wrapped in white kerchiefs crossed themselves ceaselessly and on two knees bowed their heads to the ground, submerged in waves of tourists. The chant, thunderous and delicate by turns, rose and filled the air, as did the incense. The priests came and went about the sacramental task in robes and with ceremony unchanged for centuries. The utilitarian world was excluded and ignored. From a large seminary-cum-monastery in a walled garden there occasionally emerged monks in flowing robes cleaving through the crowds without contact; but our guide dropped his numbers game and we were not told how many monks there were. With a morsel of blessed bread and a cup of water from the sacred spring outside the church I sought my sparse communion.

The village of Zagorsk is just one long street with virtually no concessions to human needs, such as food, for countless pilgrims. A species of doughnut filled with a little ball of meat bought at one street corner, a drink made of fermented black bread bought at another, was the only sustenance available.

Next morning there was the train for Leningrad – a journey of seven hours. You are not allowed to take photographs from the train window. I wonder why. In 700 kilometres or so, there is nothing to see except hillocks and shrub in a flat horizon, almost no cultivation, no sign of livestock, little huddles of houses now and then – wooden huts or two-storey bungalows, painted dark green or red, in derelict compounds. Anything like a village church or a pub is unimaginable.

Television masts are everywhere and presumably induce the official view of events at home and abroad, since there is no other.

But at the end of the line is lovely Leningrad, its name usurping that of the city of Peter the Great's realised dream. It has the grandeur, the style of a great capital city with no half-measures. The river which divides it must be the broadest in the western world. It is all of a piece with its palaces, its fortress and its churches; but it is frozen.

Its political life has been taken to Moscow, its social life killed. The ruins and depredations of revolution and war have been made good, but the whole place is a museum where nothing lives except the shades of Russia's greatest writers and the guides in endless explanation. St Isaac's cathedral is reminiscent of St Peter's in Rome, and almost as big. There is hardly an inch of wall unadorned with resplendent sacred imagery. It all looks down on an uncomprehending mob shuffling in groups under various guides. No public prayer has been uttered there for over 50 years.

In this city the hand of Peter the Great and Catherine is to be seen in every artefact. The remains of the last tsar and his family have been obliterated. 'Their tomb might have become a fetish', explained the ingenuous Intourist guide. Half a million soldiers and civilians who died in the long siege of 1941–42 are buried in common graves: mound after mound. The flame for the unknown soldier gutters over the scene, immobile sentries survey it and the Red Flag is ever at half-mast. Chopin's funeral march comes over from loudspeakers in the trees. A seemingly endless trail of tourists moves through, their threadbare religion thus preserved.

The end of the tour took us towards the docks. Here another vast hotel was rivalled in size by a general store across the way, reserved for hard-currency holders and party bosses. These buildings face the Gulf of Finland and eventually the open sea. The gulf sparkled in the sunlight. One had the sensation of looking from a high terrace to the infinite possibilities of another life. At our back was the vast land-mass of Russia, a sixth of the earth's surface. The plight of the human mass within it weighed heavily on the imagination: tyrannised in mind and body for the sake of a busted economic theory and a philosophical vacuum. Buried in this mass, we know, are truly human homes, poets and painters, writers, mystics and humble believers, but only now are they beginning to be even tolerated.

Such thoughts were inescapable as the journey ended. There were signs, of course, of some loosening up of the governmental grip on every aspect of life. Why, in my copy of *Moscow News* on that last day, there was a letter from an old war veteran urging his like to throw away all the medals which had been won under Stalin. A straw in the wind, a wind which will eventually blow away the memory of that monster. His monuments will topple, he will be diminished in the official Communist history books, 30 million people murdered at his orders will be blandly overlooked or posthumously pardoned. A different history will be imposed, a new myth created, but deep down at the heart of the whole system is a lie about its very nature, carefully fostered from generation to generation, and this will persist in a different guise so long as the system persists. The one cannot live without the other.

From where else on God's earth, in so many travels in countless countries, have I come away with such a sense of spiritual deprivation? I would dismiss it as a morbid hallucination were it without cause, but the cause is real enough. Despite the Party leader's recent effort towards a more open attitude to religion, amongst other things, the long banishment has worked.

This conviction of mine was borne out on my return as I listened to Professor Hoskins's Reith lectures broadcast on the BBC. Of religion in Russia he said, 'the Church itself has been seriously, perhaps fatally, weakened by the Party's own treatment of it. Decades of active persecution alternating with contemptuous manipulation have left it not only numerically reduced but spiritually debilitated to the extent where it may no longer be able to play the role the Party now envisages for it.' Mine was not a hallucination after all.

16

Envoi

The longest holiday had its base prepared in Spain long before it really began. On the Atlantic coast of Andalusia there is a village called Mazagon, about twenty kilometres from the port of Huelva. One day, twenty-five years ago, Mabél heard from a friend that there was a stretch of land between the coast road and the sea next to her own house that had just come up for sale at a nominal price. The temptation to investigate was irresistible. I flew from London to join Mabél in Madrid for the journey south: all night in a vintage *wagon-lit*.

There it was: about an acre of sand surrounded by barbed wire. A prospective buyer had sunk a well in the middle of it proving the existence of abundant fresh water. It was just a strip of sand but we had sovereignty within our grasp. Formerly a military zone, some clerk in a ministry had presumably written it off as no longer needed. Formalities for the purchase were easily completed, the only condition being that we build a house of a reasonably high standard. Such an operation was cheap and easy in those days. An architect friend in Madrid produced the plans, just for love, and a local contractor soon got to work.

I left the whole development of the project to Mabél. In the midst of that barren patch rose a two-storey building of logical proportions and Andalusian grace. With children and grand-children and guests in mind, she built it to sleep twelve people in comfort. It has an upper-terrace room with three sides in glass where, in fact, I have written this book. The sun shines for at least 300 days in the year, bright and pale in winter, burning hot in summer, but even then tempered by the sea breeze from the west.

The sea lies open before me: sometimes dappled with cloud-shadows, more often just moving through shades of blue as the day goes on: steel blue in the early morning, cobalt at midday and *eau-de-nile* touched with gold at sunset. Puffing fishing boats move about off shore when they are not lying on the beach like lazy sunbathers. From time to time a tanker heaves itself over the horizon, bound for Huelva. She will creep along in the lee of a great breakwater of piled-up concrete blocks stretching for seven kilometres out to sea in those shallow waters, ending in a lighthouse. In the winter storms Atlantic rollers crash against its shelter and are broken up in spray.

The road behind the house has now been metalled, lit and strung with telephone wires – nothing of which existed when we first arrived. The other chalets, each one of different design, are empty most of the year. The old sandy road has now become the *Avenida de los Conquistadores* – hardly appropriate for our mild-mannered neighbours from Seville and Huelva who only venture from their town houses in July and August. We are in walking distance of a little church on one hand and a general store on the other, so food for soul and body is not difficult to find.

Often, when we go down to the sea, there are no footprints in sight, nobody to be seen, no sound but the murmuration of the waves turning and flopping on the sand. This is Columbus land – our next village is Palos from where he set sail 500 years ago. His watering well and the church of his last prayer on land are still there. Nearby is the Franciscan friary of La Rabida which has been there since Columbus lodged with the friars deep in discussion of theology and navigation, in his case the one motivating the other. The surrounding country is covered for miles with umbrella pines, robust enough to stand against the high salt-laden winds in winter. Only behind the pine forest does Andalusia show its true colours in olive and orange groves, vines, peach trees, fields of sunflowers and all manner of other crops.

I look out from this tip of Europe towards a world that was a myth for countless centuries, unknown to Europeans. A home has sprung up decked with bougainvillaea of every colour, with its three giant eucalyptus trees at the gate, and masses of mimosa, some of it even braving the sea winds at the back of the house, where azaleas and geraniums cover the sand. We are looked after by garrulous, ever cheerful Matea whose circumference equals her height, and monosyllabic Antonio, her husband, who lends an occasional hand. For food we have abundant fish and peasant fare. The celestial light white wine of the district is easier to come by than mineral water.

It is our home for about a third of the year, for preference in spring and autumn with their long drawn-out promises of change, as against the static months of high summer. I look out at Herman Melville's 'watery world', reflecting that we are in fact on a high plateau, sloping very gently into the ocean depth. I like to think of its mountains and grand canyons, of the pitch-dark deep where giant fish and an endless variety of smaller fry girate oblivious of the outer air and of humanity's small quarter of land on the globe's surface.

There is little that must be done in the way of chores, yet plenty to do if one is so inclined: the sort of reading that is difficult in London's tempo, the sort of writing that doesn't fit with the constant interruptions of town life. I have time to paint, in a vain imitation of nature. News of the great world comes on a radio crackling with atmospheric interference and through the local press with its unique mixture of politics, *fiestas*, bullfights and pilgrimages – or *romerias* instinct with folklore. With all this Andalusia is like nowhere else on earth (except, of course, where it has succumbed to modernity, in Marbella and the like).

As I write now the swallows have arrived, non-stop from Africa; a couple have built a nest high up in an angle of the building over the *patio*, next to my balcony. They have built it by instinct but with all the ingenuity of a Swiss watchmaker, somehow sticking it safe to the bare surface of the white wall. Sometimes a rarer bird will stray from the great reserve of the Coto Doñana, a few kilometres down the coast towards Seville.

A month ago a falcon hovered incongruously over the dune; my grandsons enticed it to land and pick up a raw red Spanish sausage which it gobbled up quite close to them, glaring ferociously at its uncustomary company. Seagulls are rare except when they gather in flocks on the beach in late autumn or suddenly appear in the wake of a fisherman's trawl. Gannets seem to be summer birds, soaring and diving from high up into the water when they spot a fish. Hoopoes and magpies are the only birds that I can put a name to except for a nightingale which sings as I breakfast in the garden; it never gets used to the double summer time imposed on the country.

However closely-knit a family may be or strong the ties with friends, here one finds a personal solitude in the immensity of sea and sky and discovers that the use of memory is much more than a matter of recall, even with the discarding of the dross and negativity of the past. The more I contemplate this business of living the more do I realise that its motive and meaning for all of us is a matter of love. The very word is abused and misunderstood more than any other in our language, sentimentalised or trivialised. Nevertheless it is the lodestone of all living. We are all drawn by love: of persons above all, of our dogs and cats perhaps, of art in all its forms, of the natural world and the intricate marvels of its constituents.

The world of souls has an attraction all its own: their own world, their search and even the suffering that often goes with it. Mankind is a fellowship however much fragmented by violence at various times and places. My belief is that this human fellowship – the whole race – was created and is sustained by God and that Christ lives amongst us since Resurrection day.

I accept that this is meaningless to any atheistic philosopher, meaningless too for all those who are simply unaware of it by custom, by conceit, or for lack of any guidance. They think of it, when they think at all, as mumbo-jumbo. But even their choice implies and requires human freedom, the freedom of the creative mind which is something unique in all creation and the key witness to the existence of God, the totally gratuitous creator of all.

I see all this as I look back in wonder at the tapestry of my life. It is a jumble of multi-coloured threads and knots on one side, in my day-to-day stitching together of this and that, but on the other emerges a coherent pattern or picture of infinite variety and surprise. 'Over again I feel Thy finger and find Thee,' as Hopkins puts it. Or, as that curmudgeonly old French prophet of the nineteenth century, Léon Bloy, wrote, having been through much agony of spirit, '*Tout ce qui se passe est adorable.*'

ORDER

NEQVANDO DICANT GENTES VBI EST DEVS EORVM

VT SAPIENTES DICANTVR QVI RES RECTE ORDINANT ET EAS BENE GVBERNANT

Design by David Jones, for the cover of the magazine Order. *A unicorn prancing in an enclosed garden 'to cleanse the water'*

Index of Names